# BEULAH:

## A Biography of the Mineral King Valley of California

Great West and Indian Series, Volume 50

# BEULAH
## A Biography of the Mineral King Valley of California

## By Louise A. Jackson

Westernlore Press § Tucson, Arizona § 1988

Library of Congress Catalog Number 88-050015
ISBN 0-87026-065-0

PRINTED IN THE UNITED STATES OF AMERICA BY WESTERNLORE PRESS

In memory of Alice Crowley Jackson,
who loved and lived the legends of Beulah,
preserving its history for all of us.

# TABLE OF CONTENTS

# BEULAH:

## A Biography of the Mineral King Valley of California

---- ◆ ----

# PREFACE

The history of the Mineral King Valley is the study of a character. Its personality is as individual as the men and women who have helped to shape it. Decades of survival, of use and misuse, of struggle and solitude, have etched their patterns on its face.

Mineral King is the Sawtooth Circle, an alpine valley that lies to the west of the main crest of the Sierra Nevada in California. Its eastern face is a part of the Great Western Divide, with peaks rising to over 12,000 feet. Hanging canyons and granite cirques rise over the timbered slopes of its valley floor. There are lakes and ridges and waterfalls. There are high passes and perfect gaps. There are meadows and streams and wildlife. There is silver. There is gold.

For over a century, this valley has been embattled. It has borne constant conflict, with man's desire both to plunder and to preserve its resources.

Mineral King's story is the story of man's dreams. It is the story of Beulah, the biblical land of beauty. The land of expectation and promise. The land of perpetual hope.

*Harry's Bend, 1969—Harry Parole established his first camp in 1874 on the bend of the East Fork near the location of the cabins shown in the picture.*

# ONE

---◄◉►---

# DISCOVERY

When Harry Parole discovered the Mineral King Valley in 1862, he looked down from what is now called Farewell Gap into very nearly the same scene that you would find today. It was like no valley he had found in all his wanderings throughout the Sierra Nevada. More gentle than most, and serene in its isolation, its mountain sides held all the color Harry had ever dreamed of as a miner.

Lying far from any trade routes, there was no reason for the valley's discovery at that time. It was far above the mining belt of the foothills. The lower canyons were too rugged for trappers to work. The surrounding area of the Sierra was too remote for livestock grazing. Only because Harry Parole had a dream and an Irishman's large sense of curiosity, was it discovered in that year.

Gold was the trailblazer. Gold and silver, creating the trails that eventually would lead Harry to the gap. Until 1854 almost no one had explored the wilderness depths of the southern Sierra Nevada of California. The Indians and a few cattlemen and sheepherders knew the higher mountains, but there were no trails of any size.

The cry of gold had passed the southern Sierra by. Throughout the first great rush of 1849, after the discovery of gold at Sutter's logging camp, the long Central Valley of the tules and the southern mountains remained quiet. But gradually, a few unsuccessful miners drifted southward from the northern mines. Some came in search of new diggings, but most came to try ranching along the river deltas of the Central Valley. They settled the land and prospected the foothills in their free time, but there were no rich strikes to be found.

In the summer of 1854 the quiet was broken. Gold was discovered in the Kern River Canyon and, just a few days later, at White River. Within four months the greatest gold rush in the history of California had made its mark. Between four and five thousand men roamed the mountainsides. Towns were built and trails cut to them.

Along with all the other settlements close to the foothills, the merchants of the little town of Visalia sent pack trains of provisions to the diggings. They found it was not the money-making venture they had expected. The existing trails were so primitive and slow that the merchants realized they must quickly pool their resources and contract for a new one.

The Dennison Trail broke the wilderness. It reached every mining camp and stock range and sheep camp in the area, winding its way through the mountains to become the first trans-Sierra route from the San Joaquin Valley on the west to the Owens Valley on the east.

This was only the beginning. In 1860 silver was discovered in the Cosos Mountains of the Owens River Valley. Once again the merchants of Visalia started sending provisions across the high mountains and again they decided a better trail was needed. In 1861 and 1862 John Jordan and his sons built the trail, from Visalia to Independence. At the same time a wagon road was opened from Bakersfield over Walker's Pass into the eastern desert.

It was the beginning of the Civil War in 1861 that brought the most used trail across the southern Sierra Nevada. Again it was silver that created the need. Ore from the Cosos Mountains was being promised to the Confederacy. To protect its interest in the mines, the Union forces reactivated Fort Independence in the Owens River Valley. Immediately supplies for the desert fort's maintenance became a problem. As short as the Jordan Trail had seemed at first, a shorter trail was needed now.

Three men decided to undertake the job. On December 11, 1862, permission was granted to Bill Cowden, Lyman Martin, and John

B. Hockett to build a toll trail. The United States Government sent men from Fort Independence to help. It appointed John Hockett to supervise the construction and routing. And it hired Harry Parole, a mountain man of the area, to provide meat for the trail crews.

Harry Parole was more than just a mountain man. He was a legend. In his lifetime he had emigrated from Ireland, had roamed the United States, had finally settled near the California coastal town of San Gregorio. He had been a dock hand, a day laborer, a miner, a cattle man. But the legend of Harry Parole was as a fighter.

Harry had been champion of his county in San Gregorio, and he had been jailed more than once for his brawls. Born Harry O'Farrell, he changed his name to Harry Parole when a judge from Redwood City defeated him in a fight. Disgraced, Harry disappeared for a time. Then he reappeared at the White River gold rush. As Harry Parole, he roamed the southern Sierra, hunting, trapping fur bearing animals in the winter, prospecting in the summer, searching for a valley of gold he believed lay somewhere in the mountains. When the Hockett Trail was started in 1862 he became the trail crew's game hunter.

As the trail was built, the crew moved from campsite to campsite and Harry explored the newly opened countryside for game. When camp was moved to a point on the Little Kern River, Harry and a Paiute Indian helper went in search of new hunting grounds.

They decided to follow the Little Kern's canyon upstream. It became a steep canyon, rough, rocky, and hard to climb, and Harry considered turning back. But as he and the Indian climbed, they saw a gap ahead, formed between two peaks that looked identical in height. Harry had never seen such a perfect gap and he decided to go up and take a look.

In later years, Harry loved to tell the story of his discovery to his friends. It seemed the horses had become skittish as they neared the top of the pass, so Harry and the Indian walked them into the gap. As they reached the center, they were struck by a gale of wind that stopped abruptly only a few yards down either side of the pass.

Harry had a rugged soul, but he knew beauty. He and the Indian moved slowly down the canyon into the valley below. On the way, they met game everywhere. Deer were lying in groups under fir

[3]

trees and aspen. Some were quietly cropping grass on the hillsides. They startled slightly when the hunters approached, then continued to eat. In the shade of a grove of aspen, a flock of mountain sheep was napping through mid-day. More timid than the deer, they rose and bounded off the rise of land across the draw, and on to the mountainside beyond. Farther on, Harry heard a scrambling noise down a small ravine. Two cub bears were wrestling each other while their mother watched them from her bed of bracken fern. Harry and the Paiute passed closed by, but she did not even turn to look at them.

The floor of the valley leveled out, its gravelly soil padded with pink catpaws, sulphur flowers, and baby's breath. In the meadows and marshlands, the horses pushed their way through belly-high flowers and grasses. Grouse drummed and marmots cheeped behind tumbled boulders.

But as they rode northward, only the mountain slopes to the east held Harry's attention. Their lower portions were covered with a growth of willows and quaking aspen set in a red and yellow mineral rich soil. The two men moved along the stream past more canyons and falls until they reached the north end of the valley below a sawtoothed peak. There the stream turned sharply to the west, flowing out of the valley. Harry stopped there, and he and his Indian helper headed back up the valley, pausing just long enough to secure meat for the trail crew.

As they neared the winds of the pass, Harry turned once more to look back over the valley with its high peaks, deep canyons, and falling streams. This was it. He knew it. The coloring, the formation, all the signs were there. It was what he had been looking for. His valley of gold.

# TWO

-----◄◉►-----

# A WHITE CHIEF

For years Harry Parole kept the secret of his discovery. No one knew where he spent his summers. He would disappear for weeks at a time and when he was seen again, he would only tell his friends that he had been hunting.

He made one trip to Visalia, to the surveyor's office, and found on a map that the canyons he had discovered formed the source of the watershed of the East Fork of the Kaweah River.

Harry set up camp on the bend of the river where he and the Paiute had stopped on the day of their discovery. It was a good spot, with a boulder-free flat, a scattered group of small fir trees to give shade, and the river was near at hand. Toward the west it opened out to sunsets. To the east the sawtoothed peak caught the sun's first morning rays. To the south his valley rose up to the windy pass with the sight of high crags on every side.

Harry explored, prospected, gathered data, and dreamed. There was no free gold to be found, but indications of rich ores were everywhere. All he needed to do was to find their sources.

Finally, he decided he could not accomplish it alone. He confided his secret to one friend. One friend, then two, then little by little, the news of his discovery was whispered about. Special friends were invited to visit him and have a look. He directed them by way of the Hockett Trail, up over Farewell Gap, then down into his

[5]

*"The Gate" Harry Parole built to contain stock within the valley during the early mining days. It was located below Barton's Camp at a location now bordering Faculty Flats below the ranger station.*

valley where, at the big bend of the East Fork, they would find his camp. His friends came and they stayed. A summer settlement grew and it became known as Harry's Bend.

Other men heard about the valley, and some of them tried to find it. But without trails or directions, it was almost impossible. Some tried the East Fork Canyon by way of Three Rivers, but it was a long and hard experience. If they kept close to the turbulent river, there were high bluffs and waterfalls that in places made ascent almost impossible. To detour around them, it was necessary to break through chaparral so thick that often it could not be penetrated. Some of the adventurers looked for a way high on the north side of the canyon, going through an area of enormous trees. They ran into trouble, too, with lateral canyons, rock slides, and thick growths of underbrush. Still, a few did reach the mountain valley, leaving a slight indication of a trail. Over it came more people; adventurers, prospectors, friends; and in 1870 Matilda Crowley came, the first woman to reach Harry's Bend.

In August 1872 the future of Harry's valley was decided. Around three separate campfires, the decision was made. In that month, Harry Parole made his first real strike. He and his friend, Bill Anderson, had come upon a rock slide in one of the valley's side canyons. Scattered through it were chunks of heavy, gray-black rock, and nearby was an outcropping of the same formation. Harry had studied rocks and ores for years and he knew the signs. They were rich in galena ore, the richest appearing ore he had yet found. Harry staked out the claim and called it the "Yellow Jacket." He was going to go down to Visalia to file the claim, but he decided to wait one more day. Years before he had seen similar showings on a mountainside beyond the windy gap, in the Alpine Creek country. He and Bill decided to check them before going down to Visalia.

The two men camped near Alpine Creek, and on that evening Harry made a decision. This claim would be the first one from his land of promise, and Harry decided that it should be filed under his real name. Once again Harry would use his legal name of O'Farrell in all his business transactions. But he would still be Harry Parole to all his friends.

While on a hunting trip that same afternoon a fourteen-year-old boy and his uncle met Harry and Bill Anderson near Alpine Creek. The boy's uncle knew Harry and he knew of Harry's valley, but he had never been there. The two hunters talked with the two prospectors for a short time, then they went their separate ways. Harry and Bill Anderson went on up Alpine Creek, and the boy and his uncle went to their camp on the Little Kern.

In the evening, the young boy sat near a campfire at their camp and listened to his uncle talk about Harry Parole and his valley, about his lonely way of life, his prospecting, about his fantastic dreams and beliefs in his valley of gold. As the boy poked the fire with a long willow stick, he made a decision about his own future. On that evening, young Arthur Crowley decided that Harry Parole would not keep all that rich country for himself. Some day, part of it would be his.

And in that same month of August 1872 John Crabtree, Charles Belden, and George Loup were also camped in the Little Kern country. They had come to do a little hunting and prospecting and they, too, were discussing Harry's Bend and the potential of paying ore which Parole claimed was there. Rumors were growing about the valley and they sounded more promising as they spread. Some of the reports had actually been verified by miners who had prospected there and had found specimens of ore. Having known Parole on the White River diggings, Crabtree respected the quiet Irishman. He recalled Harry's belief that somewhere in the Sierra were hidden vast deposits of gold. His aim in life had been to find them. So perhaps these rumors of Harry's valley were true.

Crabtree and his two friends were ranchers and prospectors, but they were devout spiritualists, too. The three of them told of a startling experience they had on that moonlit August night. According to the earliest versions, this is the story John Crabtree told.

While they were sitting at their campfire on the Little Kern, a vision appeared before them. It was the spirit of a giant white Indian chief. He pointed northward and in a soft voice, told them of a peculiar place where the mountains were white and red and black. Within these mountains there were natural shafts and tunnels and caverns whose walls were interlaced with veins of gold. He told the men to saddle their horses and take the longest lengths of rope they had. Beckoning them to follow him, the white chief led the way.

They followed the Little Kern Canyon, which would have been difficult to climb in broad daylight and certainly impossible at night. But under the guidance of the white chief, the night's strange journey met with no problems at all. He led them up the western side of the canyon, above the timber line and on to steep, rocky slopes, veering their course toward some cliffs above a windy pass. They wound their way around the southern base of these cliffs toward the west. There they were stopped by a jagged, pinnacled granite wall with a sheer drop on its opposite side. They tethered the horses, then unwound the lengths of rope to scramble down the face of the wall.

[8]

J. A. Crabtree; Porterville rancher and prospector, one of the discoverers of the White Chief Mine.

(Above) *The wall the great White Chief led the Crabtrees over to the first discovery of gold.* (Below) *Entrance to the White Chief Mine, the principal mine of the New England Tunnel and Smelting Company in 1874. The 200 foot tunnel is still open.*

Reaching the base, they found themselves in a great amphitheater, a large circular canyon. The Indian spirit stood on a massive mound of granite far below them, with arms outstretched, pointing in every direction. Just as the sun rose over the eastern peaks, the great white chief faced the men, then with an upward thrust of his great arms, he vanished from sight.

Crabtree, Loup and Belden stood bewildered. This, apparently, was the place. Here was where their fortunes would be made. It was a peculiar country of white granite, quartz, and limestone, with contrasts of black and red outcroppings, and beautiful beyond compare. They walked into it and they called it "White Chief."

The three men spent the first hours of the morning exploring, picking up a few ore specimens, giving the country a quick inspection. They had difficulty in reaching the meadow at the bottom of the canyon below them. The sides were steep and filled with broken slabs and loose blocks of granite. A small stream ran through the meadow and Loup followed it until it disappeared into a cave on a hillside of white quartz. The entrance to the cave was low, but wide enough to enter. Loup stooped down, then he let out a yell and shot from the cave as though possessed. He had all but stepped on a large black bear curled up on the floor of the cave.

By mid-morning, the three men decided they should hurry back to file some claims. Returning to their horses, they built trail markers along the way of rocks piled in monument fashion. They marked their path all the way back to the Hockett Trail, making certain they would be able to return and claim the fabulous country revealed to them by the great white chief.

After that month of August 1872 Harry Parole's valley would never again be the same.

*The White Chief cabin, built in 1878. It was used as a bunk house for the miners in 1878 and 1879.*

# THREE

## BUNCO OR BONANZA

Unlike Harry Parole, Crabtree, Loup, and Beldon shared the news of their discovery with everyone they met. When they reached Crabtree's ranch near Porterville, they gathered a group of friends and organized their return to White Chief. A pack train carrying provisions and prospecting equipment was soon on its way. According to old records, J. A. Crabtree, J. P. Ford, Charles Beldon, Newton Crabtree, the Loup brothers, and Peter Goodhue, all ranchers or businessmen from the Porterville country, made up the prospecting party.

While these men were preparing to return to White Chief, Harry Parole and Bill Anderson were winding their way over Farewell Gap from Alpine Creek. The Alpine showings had looked good and now they were on their way to prospect another area that Harry had seen in his valley high on the slopes of a mountain that he had named Empire.

They spent the night in their permanent camp at Harry's Bend. The next morning while packing their mule with provisions for a few day's stay on Empire, they were interrupted by shouts up canyon. Three men rode into camp and told Harry and Bill Anderson about the White Chief discovery.

As soon as the men left, Harry and Bill decided to try to find the discovery. They saddled their horses and followed the main canyon

[13]

up toward Bearskin, to the first meadow below the white granite walls. They prospected for some time, digging, dynamiting, searching. But they found nothing that even suggested gold in quantities. They did stake out one claim just in order to prove they had an interest there. Disappointed and disgusted, they left the White Chief to Crabtree and his visions and headed back to Harry's Bend.

Word of the discovery spread life wildfire. Visalia was in a state of fever. A gold rush would mean growth, wealth, importance, and the news sent out from there was fabulous beyond belief. Fortunately, along with the exaggerated accounts of the richness of the ore, the near inaccessbility of the region was pictured too.

Still, in spite of its remoteness, there were brave souls who did dare to seek it out. By end of 1872 prospectors with their miner's eyes, their miner's picks, and their miner's hopes, were trudging unknown trails into the Sierras.

That summer Harry Parole and Bill Anderson ignored the excitement and made camp in a ridge of sheltering fir on Empire Mountain. Above them rose rugged cliffs with outcroppings similar to those found at the Yellow Jacket Mine, with huge tumbled boulders overlapping in such a way as to form caves and natural shafts. It was a barren and forbidding formation, but exciting and interesting to the two prospectors.

One day Harry stumbled onto a small opening that plunged straight down into the mountain's depths. Marking it carefully he called to Bill Anderson and they hurried back to camp for ropes and a lantern. Bill lowered Harry down the narrow shaft and at the bottom Harry lit his lantern. There, stretched before him was a large cavern with rocks of quartz strewn all over the floor. Harry sent samples up to Bill, then clambered up after them.

What he found became the mighty Empire Discovery Mine. Harry Parole and his partners, J. P. Anderson and J. A. Samstag, staked their claim to it but they did not file it until July of 1873 when they became owners of what was to be the richest and most disastrous mining venture in this land of promise.

When Crabtree's return party dropped down over the granite wall at White Chief, they saw an immediate problem. Until a trail was built, no gold could be taken out. A way must be found for stock to get over that wall. With difficulty the men circled eastward. The cliffs diminished in height until they reached a point where, with some blasting, they could be crossed. From there a trail had to be zig-zagged down the loose, bouldered mountain slopes to the meadow at its base. The men made their trail and it became the popular route thereafter used from Porterville. It left the Hockett Trail on the Hockett Meadow side of the Circle and was known as the Hockett entrance.

Crabtree and his friends explored the White Chief area and their enthusiasm grew. They laid plans for its development. They decided where a permanent mining camp would be placed, on the forested side of the large, lower meadow through which a snow-fed stream meandered. They decided where the trees would be cut for mine bracings and cabins and buildings. Then they staked out the first claim. They called it the "White Chief Mine," and began tunneling into the mountain.

Ore was there in quantity. They took it out and the assays were good in both gold and silver. But Crabtree reported that the ore in which the metals were imbedded was "difficult of extraction." It would be an expensive operation to develop mines and a mining camp. More trails and eventually roads would have to be built. Stampmills, smelters, roasters, and mining equipment would have to be obtained; sawmills erected; housing built. But these miners were undaunted. They saw through eyes of gold and silver. Tremendous wealth awaited them.

The first and most pressing need was a shorter and better access trail. Other than the Hockett entrance, there were only two inadequate routes in existence. One was by way of Dillon's Mill on the North Tule to the Little Kern and over Farewell Gap. The other was a very poor cattle trail which James Lovelace had extended from his cattle range out of Milk Ranch to Harry's Bend.

The trail-conscious merchants of Visalia again saw the opportunities that lay ahead. A short time after the opening of White Chief, $3,000 were raised. John Meadows, one of the most enthusiastic of the men who had become interested in the promise of the opening mines, was selected to supervise the building of a new trail.

Haste was necessary. The fall equinox, with its threatening

storms, was only a few weeks away and that would hold up work. Pleasant Indian summer days should follow in October, but that was uncertain. Every good day must be used to the limit if men were to grow rich that year.

The trail began at the end of the county road at Three Rivers and followed the East Fork route scratched out of the canyonside by the first adventurers seeking Harry's Bend. The East Fork resounded with the blasting of dynamite as the resistant chaparral was chopped, grubbed and burned, and granite cliffs were leveled. To build such a trail under normal circumstances would have been a discouraging undertaking. But John Meadows, with enthusiasm, determination, power of persuasion and skill, drove his crews ahead. He pushed himself harder than anyone, worked with his men wherever the task was the hardest and the most dangerous.

By the time winter set in the trail was completed to a point about six miles below Harry's Bend. There work had to stop. Most of the men returned to the San Joaquin Valley, but others stayed on and built log cabins. A small settlement was established which Meadows named "Silver City." There they waited out the winter storms and as soon as the snow melted sufficiently in the spring, trail crews rushed their work to completion. By early summer 1873 the new trail was opened for use.

Excitement and dreams of wealth knew no bounds. As early in the spring as men could break their way through the snow and reach Harry's Bend, prospectors were on their way to the discovery. After the new trail opened miners flocked in. Pack trains of mules carried heavy machinery and all the equipment necessary for the building of a mining community.

The greatest need then was for lumber to brace the mines and to supply housing. Al Weishar, of Visalia, arranged to construct a mill on a flat in the midst of a heavily forested area up the mountainside from Meadow's "Silver City" and about five mile below Harry's Bend. He hauled all the mill equipment up the new trail by mule-back. As soon as it opened, the mill ran day and night and yet could not meet the demand. Two other mills were built. One was in a stand of giant Redwoods at what is now Atwell's Mill. Later, the other, which was run by water, was erected near the Iron Spring across the East Fork, not far from Harry's Bend. As the

*Nig's Cave, named after an old black bear that lived in the White Chief area during the mining operations of the New England Tunnel and Smelting Company.*

camp grew these three mills, in continuous operation, supplied the lumber needed.

Dwellings of all kinds sprang up: from Barton's camp below the Gate, where Enos Barton built the first cabin in the valley; on up the East Fork Canyon to the bench and forested lands at the foot of Farewell; and into the flats of Eagle Lake and White Chief. It was at White Chief that the big, black bear that George Loup had discovered in the cave in the upper meadow became boss. As the White Chief camp was developed, the bear claimed it as his own. The miners called him "Old Nig," and his den is still known as "Nig's Cave." He became a nuisance, but he was a source of

[17]

amusement, fun, disorder and entertainment, and the miners accepted him.

It soon became evident that a mining district with rules and regulations must be formed. A meeting of all miners was called early in 1873, and the Mineral King Mining District was organized. Officers were chosen by those who joined it. J. P. Ford was elected recorder, which proved to be the most lucrative office. Fees from the recording of claims, locations, mill sites and transfers amounted to $6,000 in 1874. The fee for filing and recording each claim alone was five dollars. To retain their mines from year to year, miners had to re-file their claims each January, then do $100 worth of assessment work on each claim throughout the year. Otherwise, claims could be jumped or lost through default, although records show there was very little claim jumping in the district. After having maintained the required amount of work on his mining claim for a specified number of consecutive years, the miner had the privilege of applying to the United States Government for a patent.

The mountain slopes on which most mines were located were too steep to construct mills for extracting the metals from the ores. So the mine owner was granted the right to "prove up" on a mill site of five acres on the valley floor and patent it also. When a mine and mill site were patented, they became the property of the miner with no more obligations required than property taxation.

Two major points were decided at the first meeting of the district. Miners would be allowed only two animals apiece to enter and graze in the valley above the gate that Harry Parole had built; one to ride and one to pack. Even so, at the height of the mining boom, something like a thousand animals roamed the valley and canyons.

A name more suitable for the settlement than "Harry's Bend" was the second point discussed. A committee was made up of Wiley Watson, Pasqual Bequette, D. W. Edwards, and the Reverend J. P. Jones. They chose the biblical name "Beulah," the land of promise.

By fall of 1873, a year after Crabtree's discovery, more than sixty claims had been filed by nearly one hundred people, the majority businessmen and ranchers from Tulare County.

The new prospectors and miners had much to learn. Many of

them had never mined before and none of them had mined in this valley. They had to learn the rocks that made the Sawtooth Circle. There was granite, limestone, gneiss, quartzite, mica schist, slate, quartz, and diorite, the latter rock forming the dark, purplish-red outcropping that made startling contrast to the prevalent light colored formations. The miners called it porphyry.

There was the variety of ores within the rocks to be learned. Assays from five general classes showed gold and silver in various amounts. There was sulphide of lead or galena, which indicated the most promising amounts; sulphide of zinc or blende; sulphide of copper; sulphide of iron; and the arsenical ores. Lead and a small amount of antimony were detected also. An assay office was set up where the prospectors paid well to have their specimens analyzed.

There was the positioning of the ores to be learned. Nature had been helpful in this. She had scattered them in three separate zones. The richest contained gold, silver, and zinc which lay hidden at elevations along the heights of the Great Western Divide and also around White Chief and Eagle Lake. Lead, silver and zinc were found at lower altitudes on the western side of the Sawtooth Circle, imbedded in less rugged ridges and timbered slopes. Copper lay almost at the bottom of the east side of the East Fork Canyon at about the elevation of Black Wolf Falls, close to the valley floor.

There were the methods of mining to be learned. There was black powder and the new dynamite to be tamed. Because of the steep mountain slopes, prospecting and mining by running tunnels was comparatively simple. Beulah's canyons rang with the sound of dynamite blasts.

The unskilled miners handled the dynamite with complete disregard for its potential power. These men, who ridiculed and scorned the idea of danger, insisted the dynamite was not explosive without a percussion cap. They claimed it could be struck with a hammer without blowing up. It could be thrown into fire and do nothing more than burn. Burros relished it as food, so they said, and could bite into a stick without harm.

When working underground, it was customary to throw the sticks down the shaft to be caught by the workmen below. If a setting did not explode immediately or failed entirely, there were miners who dug out the cap and dynamite with a shovel, reset

*Beulah, situated at the end of the present road. Most of the cabins shown existed during the mining era, later to be destroyed in the earthquake of 1906.*

them, and tried blasting it again. There were some sad results. At that time, dynamite was the greatest power man had yet produced. But the miners had their own sense of power. Dynamite was not something to fear. The only fear was failure.

By 1874 Beulah was booming. Although it was lively, it never became a brawling mining town. Many rough men drifted in, but they found the entire district well ordered and governed. Leaders from the San Joaquin Valley settlements had arrived before the boom and, in spite of the well-patronized saloons, the camp had been under control from the start. There were fist fights and drunken brawls, but only occasional gun play, mostly for the excitement and general ruckus it created. Only two serious shootings with intent to kill were recorded in the ten years of mining. Both men missed their marks.

In summer of 1874 buildings were rising fast. The Wiley Watson/J. W. Thurmond Store, the first one in Beulah, was in operation. Three saloons had opened their doors for business, hotels were going up, and two smelters were under way.

As soon as the trail was passable in the spring, Sam "Whiskey" Smith, heading a large pack train, came blustering into camp to build a hotel. Looking the canyon over, he selected a site half way between Barton's camp and the upper end of the valley. A perfect spot, he declared, viewing Farewell Gap to the south and Timber Gap to the north, situated on a sizeable area of level land near the river, and without a sign of avalanche erosion. He would make it the center of Beulah and offer the finest accommodations in camp.

The Mineral King District was all government land, and the mines and millsites were set up under strict federal regulations. The campers' building sites, however, were not restricted or controlled in any way until much later, after the U.S. Forest Reserves were established. In 1874 a person could choose any spot he desired without permit, charge, or regulation.

Smith brought carpenters along with him, but he sent out a call for more help. Beulah was almost as excited over this hotel project as it was over the mines. The men came, to help erect the grandest building in the district.

Whiskey's plans were not small. The hotel was to be two stories high with a fancy, flat facing on the front such as buildings in the northern mining camps had. There were to be gaming tables in the main room downstairs and a bar serving the best liquor that ever flowed between a man's lips. There would be a store in it, so well stocked that if a wanted item was not there, Whiskey would get it and charge only half price including transportation. A long dining room would double as a dance hall on Saturday nights, not a rowdy dance hall, but one even the wives could come to. There would be a real chef, too, not just an ordinary cook.

Downstairs, the plans called for three bedrooms and an inside staircase going up to the second story. Upstairs, there would be four special bedrooms, the two front ones having the luxury of one window apiece. The beds would have rope springs instead of straw

*Rock Chimney Cabin, one of the better "homes" of the mining era.*

ticks and there would be hooked rugs on the floors. There would be four bunk rooms too, for miners without much money. All the other men could wear themselves out digging and tunneling into the mountainsides, but Whiskey was willing to bet his hat that more gold and silver would pass through his money till than any miner would ever see.

The hotel was completed at the fantastic cost of eight thousand dollars and the final touch was added. A large sign was hung on the front facing of the building, on which was painted in large, black letters, "SMITH HOUSE." Eventually several two-story hotels were built, but Smith House was by far the most pretentious of them all, the most popular, the center of the mining camp, and without a doubt the only true bonanza of the mining rush.

After Smith House opened, that portion of the valley built up

*Smith House, built in 1874 by Sam "Whiskey" Smith. This was the largest hotel in the valley and the center of activities in Beulah.*

more rapidly than did other parts. It became known as Beulah proper. Other camps retained their old situations and names, while a few new ones were added. There were Barton's Camp, Harry's Bend, Sunny Point, the remote White Chief Camp at Lower White Chief Flat, and Ford's Camp.

J. P. Ford, the mining district recorder, did not approve of the name Beulah for a mining camp. So he left Beulah proper, and established his own area on the soda flats near the junction of Franklin and Farewell canyons, and he called it Mineral King. He built an imposing cabin of logs and all the other essentials for a popular camp, but the miners stuck with Beulah. His area was always called simply Ford's Camp.

These outlying camps were all small centers supplying needs for settlers in those areas. However, cabins were strung up and down the canyon on both sides of the river. Some were in sheltered timber protected locations, some in open spaces at the base of steep slopes, regardless of how susceptible they might be to snow slides.

It was at Beulah Camp where all the excitement was found. News reached there first. Mail arrived there for distribution. An assay office read the ores. Entertainment and liquor flowed unrestrained.

The rising cabins were built of roughly finished lumber; logs, shakes, clapboards, board and battens. Among them were dwellings much better than the usual miners' shacks. Some were built to house the families of miners who spent the summer months at Beulah, escaping the heat in the San Joaquin Valley. Some of these people considered Beulah their permanent home and lived there most of the year, leaving only during the storm-ridden months of winter.

Beulah was a silver camp. Gold had dropped in value, but silver soared in price. One early account described the prospectors as being "actually silverized." As Beulah grew and new portions of the district opened up, names were attached to different places. The peaks, canyons, gorges, rivers and lakes all received names, making them more personal to those who lived there. Most of them have retained their original names, but some of them have been changed.

Miner's Peak changed without plan or effort. It so definitely resembled a saw's tooth that to look at it was to call it "Sawtooth." Little Matterhorn, because of its similarity in shape to the famous peak in Switzerland, remained such until recent years when maps came out with the designation "Mineral Peak." For years the location of mining claims in the area was determined by using Little Matterhorn as a point of description. There was a sophistication to the name which the miners liked, something in common with the Alps, which they considered a close second to the Sierra Nevada.

Changes were not pleasing to the early mountaineers. They liked the familiarity of the old. Besides, they had taken part in bestowing the original names. Silver Lake, nestled high in the Great Western Divide south of Sawtooth, was an almost perfect cirque filled with water reflecting a silvery surface from the light gray granite peaks enclosing it. The miners felt a deep affection for this lake that symbolized the silver of their dreams. The long

[24]

streamer of water flashing down the steep mountain canyon below it, seemed to be bringing a flow of shining metal to the valley below. It seemed a desecration to the old timers to change Silver Lake and Silver Creek to "Crystal Lake" and "Crystal Creek."

Potato Row Mountain had particular significance. When early arrivals first came to Beulah, they saw beyond Black Wolf Falls a serrated mountainside with deep, slick, granite covered furrows between ridges that were topped with juniper and firs. They did not hesitate to liken it to a giant potato patch, for these men were potato conscious. It was a camp staple they never seemed to lack. Potatoes were at every meal; breakfast, dinner, and supper. Often, just potatoes alone—they had saved many a weary man from the pangs of hunger. So, these rows of hanging canyons above the valley suggested to them a potato patch, and Potato Row Mountain it became, until some people started calling it "Half Potato Row." Now both terms are used.

There have been other changes made. If the early miners were rightfully accused of being "silverized," it can just as truly be said of the later name changes that they were "mineralized," with Mineral King, Mineral Queen, Mineral Peak, Mineral Ridge all taking the place of other names.

As the year 1874 rolled along, Beulah reached a population of 500 people and hundreds of mines were being worked. No one was idle. Jobs were available at good wages and the camp was filled with activity from early morning until far into the night. Though mining was difficult and the physical labor debilitating at the high altitudes, the men could accept the hardships, for everyone was a millionaire in his own mind, and they could drink off their weariness at night.

This way of life led to one of the most profitable businesses in the mining district. Each day, the young boys who spent the summer at Beulah would take long, forked sticks and flour sacks and strike out for a marshy bog across the river from Smith House. There they waded into the mud and water, jabbing their sticks into hummocks of marsh grass, digging round clumps of rocks, gouging under tangled growths of willow roots until their clothes were mud and they were soaked to the skin.

And the catch? Rubber boas. Small, mud-colored, two-headed snakes that appeared to be only half stuffed, repulsive but harmless. They were "two-headed" because of the replica of the head imprinted on the end of their tails. And their worth? The very lives of the miners. Drinking bad whiskey at a high altitude could bring a fast attack of delirium tremens, and only the rubber boas could save a man from the shakes and hallucinations. The snakes were carried in a pocket, or, if small enough, inside the shirt or long underwear next to the skin. Their power was especially good if they were very small and had a good head marked on the tail.

The snakes sold from one to five dollars apiece. In some instances, they brought ten dollars if they were small and showed a good rear head and if the miner could raise the money. All sales were cash on the spot. The miners had great faith in the rubber boas and it was difficult for the "snake boys" to meet the demand. By the end of the summer, many of the boys had sizeable bank accounts from their efforts. Quite a contrast to the mining men who gambled on their properties, living on money they borrowed to put into the mines, planning on riches from their claims to reimburse them later on.

The yellow spillings of the miner's "coyote hole" diggings spread out over the mountainsides in increasing numbers. But no one was making money. The cost of extracting the ore was so great that no individual could make anything out of it. Finally, groups of men gathered around the campfires and in the saloons at night and decided they must work together. Mining companies would have to be formed and, like the silver interests in Nevada and northern California, there should be sale of stock, articles of incorporation, all the legalities.

In 1873 there arrived Mr. James Morgan with Mr. W. H. H. Hart and the New England Tunnel and Smelting Company. Mr. Morgan was a mining promoter from the Nevada Comstock and he organized and financed the company. Mr. Hart was a young lawyer from San Francisco, who was later to become Surveyor General of California. He ran the company. Within a year from the day George W. "Bally" Brown announced to his mining friends that he was bringing a big company into Mineral King, Hart and the New

England Tunnel and Smelting Company had gained control of most of the mining interests in the Mineral King Mining District.

The name of the company was not the only thing that was big about it. The stock valuation was listed at $10 million, and a company of that size had to do big things. W. H. H. Hart started in a big way. He looked at the trail that had just been built up the East Fork Canyon of the Kaweah River and decided that he could do better. It was a tortuous trail and and there were rumors that because it had been built at cost per mile, the contractor had intentionally made it as long as possible, with as many kinks and turns as possible.

In 1874 Hart sent a crew of Chinese workers to straighten it into a road. At one point, at River Hill, they straightened it into a 42 per cent grade. The pitch was so steep that horses could pull a loaded wagon only about the length of the rig before resting. Even with all passengers out and hiking up on foot, it could take a team three hours to make the short distance of the grade, about one and a half miles.

While the road was being completed to Cain's Flat, the machinery and equipment for a smelter were being hauled up the trail on mule-back and assembled at Beulah by more Chinese labor. "Bally" Brown became superintendent of the works. James P. Ford was named manager of the company and acted as head carpenter. An assay office was set up and the N.E.T. & S. Co. was in business.

The prospectors flocked to have their samples assayed. The readings were high. They rushed back to the canyons and mountainsides, and at a feverish pace, made more claims and bought others. The New England Company watched and bought the diggings that looked good. Many of the prospectors bought interest in the company or they sold their claims in exchange for stock.

Work began. The company bonded the White Chief Mine for $300,000. A water-run sawmill was constructed near the Iron Springs, as was a smelting furnace, a large boarding house, and other buildings. A trail was made to the White Chief Mine and a tunnel was started, which was to be a mile long and would extend to the eastern wall of the mineral belt. The company started packing out tons of ore which it promised to pay for at a rate of $5 per ton.

For two years the company performed a tremendous amount of

labor. But slowly the population of Beulah realized that nothing seemed to really have been accomplished. Then the truth came to light. The New England Tunnel and Smelting Company was in financial trouble. The company had traded so many shares of stock for unpaying claims that they had no cash on hand. A 10 cent per share assessment on the "non-assessable" stock was levied. Most of the miners who had taken stock for their claims could not, or did not want to pay. Trust in the New England Company was not what it had been. However, their shares were sold at auction and the company was in business again.

Hart and the bigger shareholders decided a new man was needed to give the company a boost. In September 1876 "Bally" Brown was replaced as superintendent by Charles Baker. In October the sawmill was operating successfully and smelting operations were resumed. A second 10 cents per share assessment was levied to bring cash for operations and then, as expenses soared, a 25 cent assessment.

The local Visalia and Porterville prospectors were confounded. Almost all sold out, and talk began to spread of the big swindle that was taking place. Almost nobody liked Baker. He was a "foreigner" from San Francisco. He had too much power over the operations of a company that had in good part been financed by the locals. And there still seemed to be no real progress on the mines.

Construction on the road was stepped up. Lumber from the sawmill poured into more buildings. Ore from several of the mines piled up outside the smelter—there was where the real trouble began.

Enos and Orlando Barton both worked for the company and Orlando later wrote about what had taken place. "In the first place, they had a man by the name of Bevins to construct the smelter and smelt the ore, and I think he was a man with lots of experience and good sense. We all had lots of confidence in him and I believe if he had been let have his way he would have made bullion easy enough, but he wasn't allowed to have his way.

". . . We started up the smelter and ran the raw ore through it three days. We run through some 30 or 40 tons, enough to give it a fair test. Then we shut down and cleaned out the smelter and put it in good shape for making bullion. Bevins said to the boss (a man by the name of Baker) that he needed about one-half ton of lead to start with, but Baker would not get it for him. Then Bevins said he could make bullion without it, but it would be harder work to get the bullion started separating from the slag. So when Bevins said everything was ready we built up a fire in the smelter and started up. You bet we were a happy gang. We were going to make bullion in Mineral King in a few hours.

"But we reckoned without the boss. He did not want bullion just yet. He knew that if we made bullion the value of the stock would immediately increase and that is what he didn't want until he could get a lot more of the stock himself. . . ."

Bevins and his crew heated the smelter and Baker turned it off. Bevins resigned without pay. Orlando and the crew tried to make bullion without Bevins ". . . as near as we could remember how Bevins had told us was right and we soon had the slag running as fine as could be. Then we began to get ready to tap the bullion pan." Baker stopped them again.

"He rushed up to the man who was feeding and told him to put in more ore and not so much coal and flux and he picked up some chunks of ore as big as his head and chucked them into the smelter and it was only a few minutes until it was frozen up solid."

Baker found a new man in San Francisco to run the smelter, but Orlando didn't think he knew anything about it. ". . . Anyway, he started up and run our roasted ore all through and dumped it down the bank without ever getting a particle of bullion. He never got it started to separating at all and that was the last effort ever made to smelt ore by the N.E.T. & S. Co. But John Crabtree, Joe Palmer and some others built a small furnace with two blacksmith bellows and melted several pounds of bullion from the slag that fellow threw down the bank."

It was no longer the New England Tunnel and Smelting Company. Now it was the "New England Thieving and Swindling Company." In its two years of full operation, not one cent had been paid for the ore that was brought out of the mines. The "mile long" tunnel at White Chief was driven no more than 200 feet. Only two small efforts had been made to smelt any ore. The employees had lost $7,000 dollars due them for wages. Those who had paid the first assessments on their shares had gotten nothing.

Baker still tried to salvage some part of his position. Claiming that transportation was the biggest problem, he pulled the tunnel workers out of the White Chief Mine and set them to work on the road instead. If the ore could not be reduced in Mineral King, then once the road was finished, it would be hauled down to the San Joaquin Valley where a better smelting operation could be built. But the directors of the company objected. They came from San Francisco to the mines and discharged Baker. They made accusations against him and against Bevins and the local stockholders, but they made no attempt to re-open operation of the smelter.

The creditors watched and listened, read the company reports in the newspapers, and they decided it was no good. In September 1877 Watson and Thurman, storekeepers at Beulah, attached the company's property and bankruptcy followed.

The dreams were crushed. In the summers of 1877 and 1878 Beulah Camp was almost deserted. Parole and Crabtree still prospected. J. H. Trauger, another of the original prospectors, still did some work on the White Chief Tunnel. Men with their families came to escape the summer heat in the San Joaquin. Some still roamed the mountainsides, staking claims in their sardine cans and tobacco tins. But the fever had died.

In fall of 1877 one last try was made. The trustee of the bankrupt company ordered work to be done around the clock, all winter long. J. H. Trauger was made superintendent of the operations. The snows were very heavy that year. By February, the company barracks and most of the other buildings were buried. Food and warmth became more of a concern than the operations of a mine.

On February 18 disaster struck. A snowslide thundered down the mountainside into the bunk house. Six employees and Harry Trauger's wife were inside. The building was crushed and one man was buried and had to be dug out. He was trapped under a desk and had resolved to shoot himself with his pistol rather than smother. Two men in a nearby cabin were injured and Mary Trauger administered aid to them until they could be taken down to Visalia. The Traugers and the remaining men braced themselves and their cabins and waited out the rest of the stormy winter. But their efforts could not keep the company alive.

The questions continued to be asked. Were W. H. H. Hart,

Charles Baker, and the other directors of the New England Tunnel and Smelting Company really swindlers? Or were they just blundering dreamers? Nobody knew. But one thing had been learned. Mining in the Mineral King district took money, and the men who had rushed to the valley were rich only in their dreams. A company had come and had failed and all that was left were the dreams.

*John W. Crowley, 1877; Visalia businessman, builder of the toll road into Mineral King, early promoter, owner of several mining interests and businesses in the valley.*

# FOUR

## THE MIGHTY EMPIRE

Harry Parole would not be discouraged. He built a cabin on his bend of the river at the north end of the valley and spent weeks prospecting, hunting, and staking out claims. Most of his time was spent in the tunnel on Empire Mountain. He took ore from it down to Visalia, showing friends, searching for a grubstake.

Then one day he disappeared. When he returned, his friends learned that he had sold his Empire claim and had gone to San Francisco. He had gone to the city to spend his fortune. He had drunk and brawled, had bought lavishly and lived high. He had stayed until all of his money was gone. Then he returned to Visalia, and finally, to his cabin at Harry's Bend. Harry stayed at his cabin for only a few days. Then he loaded a pack burro, headed up through the winds of Farewell Gap, and down into the back country of the Kern.

Money was not Harry's goal. He was not a man to covet possessions. The search was his life. To fish, to hunt, to prospect, to dream, these were his fulfillment. It did not hurt to leave his Empire Mine to Mr. Thomas Fowler. The whole Sierra was Harry's possession. It was his Empire. He needed no other.

*Matilda Crowley, second wife of John W. Crowley, in 1870 the first woman to enter the Mineral King Valley.*

The Honorable Thomas Fowler had already built an empire. Born in County Down, Ireland, in 1829, he emigrated to New York when he was 14 or 15 years old. He stayed in the East for a few years, but the idea of the frontier excited him. He tried Canada, then Texas, then headed for California with a drove of cattle. California captured him and he stayed.

Tom Fowler chose to build his home in Tulare County at a time when there were only 18 settlers and the Indians were still killing an occasional white man. He made two trips into Mexico for more cattle, then fattened them on his ranch and drove them over to the State of Nevada for the Washoe mines. He bought land, 25- or 30,000 acres, in the southern part of the state. In 1869 he had 50,000 head of cattle. He made and spent money, on land and cattle and on a little gambling. "In 1868, I was Grand Marshal of the Democratic Torchlight Procession in San Francisco," he wrote in his deposition in later years. "I lost about $40,000 in the Seymour fight."

Fowler loved politics. In 1869 he was elected to the California State Senate and served a four year term. He lost re-election by just 53 votes. Then he was elected again, only to lose his seat when the new state constitution was adopted and he was legislated out.

Tom Fowler was an energetic man. Tied to the land and cattle empire he was building, excited over his successes and his profits, he was exuberant in his roll of prestige as pioneer politician of a new state.

In 1877 he began to dream of a new empire. Living on his Antelope ranch near Visalia, he had watched the rise and fall of the New England Tunnel and Smelting Company and the death of a bonanza with its failure. But the gold and silver were still in Mineral King. All that was needed was the capital. Tom Fowler was never afraid to spend money.

The New England Company had failed with the White Chief Mine, but there were others that they had never tried to develop. In 1878 Tom Fowler bought the Empire Mine from Harry O'Farrell, J. A. Samstag and Bill Anderson for a price quoted by the county recorder as $23,000, by Fowler as $50,000. The assays were good. Where the ore brought out of the White Chief Mine had assayed at an average of $25 to $42 per ton in gold, the deposit of

[35]

ore in the natural cave of Empire showed $250 to $400 per ton of silver. Tom Fowler could see another Comstock.

Visalia was excited again. Its 3,000 residents talked on the street corners and in their homes and decided there was no doubt. Fortunes were waiting in Mineral King to be brought out. If anyone could bring them out, Tom Fowler could. He had never failed at anything. He had never swindled anyone. He had never gone into anything that he wasn't sure would bring him money.

Everyone in town had heard the story of why Tom wanted to make a new fortune. He was going to send all that he made from his mine to his native Ireland. He was going to buy his people from the rule of the British. When you knew Tom Fowler and you knew Mineral King, the idea was less than preposterous.

Tom had no trouble getting help. In San Francisco, he had friends who believed in him no less than did the people of Visalia. He formed the Empire Gold and Silver Mining Company with 100,000 shares of stock, and sold about 2,000 of them at $10 a share. He hired James Fleming, an experienced man from the gold mines of Amador County, to be superintendent. But he made certain that the mine would remain his. He controlled the company and directed all of its operations.

A work force of 30 men was sent up to the mine in that fall of 1878. The natural cave of Empire extended into the limestone about 100 feet, but it had to be reached by lowering a man down a rope. Fowler had his men drive a short tunnel into the cave and then started a lower tunnel to tap the ledge of ore several hundred feet below the surface.

He found a 15-stamp quartz mill in Grass Valley and, although he was advised by some mining men that it was only good for working free milling ore, it looked to be a good piece of equipment so Tom bought it. Then, once again, a familiar problem raised its head—transportation.

The people in Visalia had already decided in 1873 what a mining boom might mean to them. Now it looked like a real one was on the way. When Tom Fowler came down from Mineral King and told his friends that he needed a road into the mining district, they were ready. Merchants, ranchers, politicians, all paid their share for subscriptions to build it. J. W.Crowley received a franchise from Tulare County granting him permission to build the road. He formed the Mineral King Wagon and Toll Road Company, collected the funds to build it, and organized the work to be done.

If John Crowley had never built a road before, he had proved himself in other ways. Cattle rancher, storekeeper, ice delivery man; notary public, insurance agent, bank cashier, bank director; country treasurer, railroad treasurer, undersheriff; owner of a flour mill, the Visalia water works, a hotel and a restaurant; there was almost nothing in Tulare County that John Crowley hadn't tried; yes, even prospecting.

He knew the area. He and his sons had hunted in the foothills of the Kaweah for years. In August 1870 he, one son, and his new wife, Matilda, had worked their way up to Harry's Bend. In 1874 during the first mining rush, he had sent his two sons and one daughter up to Mineral King for the summer. This was at a time when a more cautious man might try to keep his children away from such an atmosphere.

Like Fowler, he had never seemed to fail at anything. Ill health plagued him, but still he led a productive life and was a highly respected and successful businessman.

The years 1878 and 1879 were bad for California, but it was a good time to build a road. There was drought and there was depression and there was no problem in finding labor. Crowley hired an average of 200 men that summer and paid them each $20 per month with board. As his son said, "We could have hired 10,000 at that price if we had needed them." At the base camp of the road, job seekers were a constant nuisance.

John Crowley and his son, Arthur, put nearly $10,000 into building the road. Fowler claimed that he put $100,000 into it. On the afternoon of March 19, 1879, work was started. Two main camps were set up. The base camp started at Cain's Flat where the New England Tunnel and Smelting Company's road had stopped. The other camp started at Mineral King. The two crews worked toward each other, blasting through granite, fighting small canyons, gullies, creeks, and the steep walls of the East Fork itself, pushing out sandy soil that fell down onto the road's path as quickly as it was shoveled away. Each crew made wagers as to how

[37]

far they could move each day, which one would complete the most miles of work. John Crowley acted as superintendent as it started, but his other businesses suffered. T. C. Mayon took his place on the road and Crowley directed the work from Visalia.

Crowley's son, Arthur, had been ill for nearly three months and he persuaded his father to let him go up on the road to see if the mountain air would cure him. It not only cured him, it made him one of the most enthusiastic prospectors there.

Six years before, Arthur had been camping with his uncle on the Little Kern and had vowed to have some part of Harry Parole's country for himself. Now he acted as time keeper on the road and his payment was not money, but stock in the corporation.

Like many of the early pioneers of our country, Arthur Crowley felt the excitement and importance of opening the land. Each event was an adventure worth recording. Each day was an event in itself. Arthur Crowley kept a diary. He took it with him to his job on the Mineral King road, to record the adventure of each day.

### Diary, 1879 — Mineral King Wagon and Toll Road

June 22, Sunday—Today is my 21st Birth-Day. Turner and Clotfelter are moving our camp to Trauger's place today. Wages were raised today to $1.00 per day.

Monday, June 23—Mr. Mayon went to Mineral King this afternoon. I went up to Doherty's camp and got the time of the men—Tom Jordan went down today—he gave me an interest in the "Little Giant" and also a lot in Mineral King.

Tuesday, July 1—Received a letter from J. J. Mack stating a large fire in Visalia, wanting father to come down—I went to the mines this afternoon—went up to Father's claim on the Empire.

Friday, July 4—All hands at work today at all camps except a few stiffs who wanted to celebrate on Johnson's "best."

Monday, July 7—We all stayed at the mines last night. Father and Uncle went up to the "Empire" this morning—I recorded a claim on the "White Wolf" this morning, a discovery claim.

Saturday, July 12—Mr. Fowler and his son Emmet arrived at our camp about 11 a.m. Mr. Fowler, Mr. Mayon, Emmet and I went up to Harry's camp for supper and got two mules for Mr. Fowler to ride to the mines.

[38]

*Ashel Loup; early prospector and resident of Beulah; brother of George Loup, one of the discoverers of the White Chief Mine.*

Wednesday, July 16—The Blasters are in Slap-Jack—the Graders over the point into Redwood—the plowers and scrapers near where the road crosses the Lovelace trail—Palmer is between two streams of High Bridge Creek.

Thursday July 24—Mr. Fowler and Mr. Halladie came to our camp this evening and stayed over night—they are on their way to the mines to make arrangements to put up a wire Ropeway from the Empire mine to the mill below.

Saturday, July 26—went to M. King this afternoon, got registered. Voted for G. Carrington for recorder—there was a private party this eve at Mr. Hoy's.

Tuesday, July 29—Large fire in the mountains west of M. King.

Thursday, July 31—Father and Ma came down this morning on their way to Visalia. His assay office is about completed.

Friday, August 1—Cooks had a big row this evening, four of them quit, whiskey the trouble as usual.

Sunday, August 3—I went to M. King this morning—Buildings are going up very lively. A crowd of young folks went up to the "White Chief" today.

Wednesday, August 6—Mr. Fowler, Beal and Mr. Coleman, the man who is superintending building the tramway, arrived in camp on their way to Mineral King. Mr. Baker commenced surveying the route for the Tramway yesterday morning and work will be commenced on it immediately.

Friday, August 8—Mr. Mayon came down from the mines—Father came down and stayed all night. After supper we took Mr. Fowler's Buck-board over Redwood Canyon.

Saturday, August 9—Mr. Mayon and I hitched up Fowler's team and started up the road, met Mr. Fowler at Doherty's old camp. He and Mr. Coleman got in and rode up to the mines. Father, Mr. Mayon and I went along with them—Mr. Thos. Fowler and Mr. Coleman are the first men that ever rode into Mineral King in a carriage of any kind, they arrived at the store of Davidson at about 5 minutes past one p.m. There is a dance tonight in Taylor's new building—the town is being surveyed by P. Y. Baker.

Sunday, August 17—After noon I hitched up and drove through

[40]

to M. King, it being the first 2-horse wagon ever droven into M. King, two light wagons followed me through.

Wednesday, August 20—Made out orders for all men employed on the road—Just 5 months from time of starting to work on it. George Dailey and Sam Evans came to camp this evening loaded with machinery for the mill of the Empire mine.

They were lined up waiting, 150 outfits camped at Redwood Canyon, waiting for the road to officially open for traffic. They came from Visalia and Tulare and Porterville, hurrying to be among the first to unload their gear in a spot they had chosen in Beulah. They rolled in a steady line up the dry foothills and over the dusty heat of Red Hill, their hame bells ringing a monotonous symphony. They took the steep plunge down to the East Fork and then waited to go up the old River Hill Grade. The teams strained and stopped under their heavy loads on the grade. The animals were cursed and beaten, but some of them would not go. There was no room to pass, so only one wagon could go up at a time. If one failed, it had to back down, draw to the side of the road and lighten its load, losing its place in the line while another wagon tried. Then on up to the cool of the first trees and Redwood Canyon, where the wagons crowded together on the mountainside until the last few yards of road were ready.

On the morning of August 21 the rush started. The machinery for the Empire Mill; merchandise and outfits for saloons, stores, restaurants, hotels; miners with their supplies; families; even preachers. The dust churned in the new road path. Wagons creaked. Horses balked. Everyone was shouting and coughing and choking, but no one pulled out. They rolled into Mineral King and celebrated with a dance. There were two fiddles and a dulcimer for music, and almost no women. But there was plenty of "Johnson's Best" in Whiskey Smith's saloon and in some of the wagons that had just come up. It was a real celebration.

The road tolls were high. One man, 50 cents; wagon and one span of animals, $2; pack animals, 25 cents each; loose horses, 10 cents each; sheep, hogs, goats, 10 cents each; buggy drawn by one horse, $1.50; additional trail wagons, 50 cents each.

But if the prices were high, they did not keep the road from being a success. On August 22 Arthur, his job completed, started down for Visalia. He passed 22 loaded teams on the way. Business was brisk all through the fall.

John Crowley had succeeded in another venture. The road had been completed in only five months and a half a day from the afternoon it was started. There were still some rough places in it. The 42 percent River Hill Grade was still a problem, and the whole road really was not much more than a widened trail. But it was there and the people were coming. Beulah was in business.

Fall of 1879 was the busiest season thus far for Mineral King. It was not just a mining district in that year; it was a city. Visalia listed its own population at 3,000 souls, and Beulah was said to have just as many. It was reported that 1500 men showed up for work at one time in the mines. When the vote was held throughout California on May 7 for the new State Constitution, nearly 500 votes were cast in the Mineral King Mining District.

The atmosphere had changed, too. The mining district that, with a feeling of religious destiny, had called its principal settlement Beulah was no longer the same—3,000 gold and silver seekers were not that religious. In 1879 the recorder of the district still had his official stationery letter-headed "Beulah," but the name had no appeal to the prospector and his way of life. Barton's, Ford's Camp, Beulah Camp, Dog Town, all were separate settlements. But the whole area was Mineral King, and little by little, the valley became known by that name.

Tom Fowler built his boom well. With much determination, a great deal of work, even more money, a town, county and state full of friends, a temperament and need for success, a little good luck, a high display of optimism, and a few theatrics for flavor, Tom was making another Comstock.

He was up and down the road all that summer, checking it, checking his Empire Mine and the progress made on it, and on the White Chief Mine. Before the road was completed he had Arthur Crowley and some of the road crew carry his shining black buck-board across the 600 unfinished yards of mountainside. The next morning he hitched his two matching blacks to it again and rode triumphantly into Mineral King as the builder of a great bonanza must, the first man to bring a rig all the way from Visalia to "his" valley.

Among the first wagons up the road were the five loaded with mining machinery for the Empire. The smelter was completed in December 1879. This was about as far as the New England Company had gone in all its two years of promises; work on the road, a smelter up, tunnels being dug. But for Tom Fowler, it was only the beginning. As he rode up and down the steep slopes of Empire Mountain that summer, he knew that a trail to the mine was not the answer. Getting the ore down to the road by mule would be too slow and too costly. Once again, he thought big.

Fowler went to Andrew Hallidie, originator of the San Francisco cable car, and hired him to design one of his wire ropeways that had been used in the northern California mines. Then he had the pieces of the Hallidie tramway brought up the mountain and installed.

It was an endless wire cable, two miles in length, that passed around an eight foot iron wheel at the mill on one end, and another at the mine a mile away. It was fitted with large iron buckets, and the weight of the ore going down pulled the empty buckets up the other side. There was a passenger car on it too, and also a lumber carrier. Huge timber supports carried the weight of the tramway at intervals of 200 feet. It was a tremendous undertaking, and one report claimed it cost Fowler $10,000 to put it into operation.

If the tramway was not to be too long, the mill site had to be within a mile of the mine. But it also had to be on flat ground, and that was not easy to find on Empire Mountain. A friend of Fowler's, as everyone was his friend, had one piece of good land within distance. Mark Lavelle told Tom he could use the land around his Cedar Point Mine. Fowler sent up a crew of workmen to build the foundation for the stamp mill, and after the road was opened and the pieces of machinery brought in, construction was started. T. C. Mayon, who had acted as superintendent of the road construction, had proved to be a good man. Fowler made him superintendent of the mill.

He sent another crew of men to Timber Gap to cut lumber and timbers for the mines and mine buildings. Another crew cut a road from the mine to the gap to bring the lumber down. They built one

Sam Belden; businessman, promoter of several Mineral King mining interests and brother of Charles Belden, also one of the discoverers of the White Chief Mine.

log cabin near the Empire, 80 feet long and 20 feet wide to be used as a store, boarding house and bunk room for the miners. Sheep and cattle were driven up the road and slaughtered for the men's meals.

The tunnels lengthened within the Empire and the ore began to come out. It rode the creaking buckets down the tramway to the mill site and piled up inside the ore bin. Everything was working well.

Fowler's was not the only mining enterprise in the district that year. No sooner had he bought the Empire than other new mining companies sprang into existence. The McGinnis Gold and Silver Mining Company; the North Extension Gold and Silver Mining Company with the amount of capital stock actually subscribed by the directors—$5 million dollars; the White Horse Consolidated Gold and Silver Mining Company with $3,450,000; the Crystal Consolidated Gold and Silver Mining Company with $5 million dollars. The money came from Visalia and the other Central Valley towns, but also from San Francisco. This was big business.

There were several promising mines. The Empire and White Chief were not the only ones that showed high assays in gold and silver. The Cherokee, Comanche, Chihuahua, the White Horse and McGinnis mines did too. There were showings of good silver at the lower elevations in the Lady Alice, Dolly Vardan, Chickasaw and Fernleaf mines. And on the east side, close to the valley floor, there was copper in the Anna Fox, the Black Wolf, Copper King, and the Tonopah.

And there were other diggings everywhere. Rust and gold colored tailings dotted the valley's walls. Every inch of the area was explored. Tents, cabins and houses spread the length of the valley and were as scattered on the hillsides as the diggings were. There were 600 houses counted, all the way from the Gate, into the timber below Farewell Gap, and up into White Chief Flat. They were built without regard to landslides or snowslides. Mines were often dug above them and the falling of rocks became such a problem that an ordinance was passed in the district requiring each man to keep his rocks on his own land.

The houses and cabins were as varied in size and comforts as were the people who occupied them. Most often, what could be built in a day or two was what sprang up throughout the valley. They were one room shacks with low, steep, four-sided roofs and one door and no windows. Or for summer use, tents did just as well and were even faster to put up, saving the precious time that could better be put into the diggings.

Those cabins used by families during the summer months were larger and more comfortable. In general, they were all built after the same plan. The floor rested on a foundation of good sized rocks, and the frame was built of logs, shakes, or clapboard. There were three rooms with an attic for bunks. The largest room was living room, bedroom, kitchen and dining room, all in one. It had a fireplace that was used for both heating and cooking. Up one wall was a very steep ladder or simply cleats protruding from the wall, making access to the attic. The roof was steep so that in the attic a person could stand up only in the very middle. The space for bunks or bedrolls depended on the size of the cabin.

The Ford, Samstag, and Oaks cabins were exceptional. The Oaks cabin had a living room and two bedrooms, with walls covered with newspapers for insulation. There was a separate lean-to kitchen, a long front porch, and a stable attached to the house.

Not everyone worked in the mines, although most did at least part of the time. There were six two-story hotels to be run, as well as 13 restaurants, 13 saloons, three butcher shops, three assay offices, and several merchandise stores. E. Rowland raised cattle, hogs and turkeys on his ranch near Springville, then slaughtered them, packed them on his burros or donkeys, and took them over the trail to Mineral King where he operated one of the butcher shops. After hours, he played his violin for dances.

There were three lumber mills, the stamp mill, retort works, blacksmith shop, coal house, and even a warehouse. Arthur Crowley helped run his father's assay office after he completed his work on the road, and he also ran a delivery wagon, charging $1 a trip, ". . . no difference how far or how big the load." Within a few days, business was so good that several other wagons took up the idea and Arthur abandoned that enterprise. He returned to his assays, following a prescription tacked above the work counter: "Silver and Gold Assay—1 tablespoon each, dried Borax and soda, and mix thoroughly with 120 grains ore, ½ oz. litharge and small quantity

[46]

*Nelson Harlan of the Cherokee Mine.*

coal—cover with tablespoon full of salt, and if much sulphur in ore, add an iron nail in crucible, then place in furnace and leave in until boiling has entirely ceased—then pour, and as soon as cool separate button from slag, and cupel."

The stage and mail service was another big business. Daily mail service was in operation the year round. Normally it came from Visalia on the stage. But when winter storms arrived sleighs were used, and then when the snow got too high, it was brought in on snow shoes.

Three six-horse stages left Visalia and three others left Mineral King every morning. They made the 60 mile trip in one day, the up rigs stopping to let the down ones go by in a cloud of dust and confusion. The horses were changed at Three Rivers, Cain's Flat, and Trauger's. One stage each way carried mail and small items, one carried passengers and whiskey, and one was a fast freight carrying about 1500 pounds at a charge of six cents per pound. Business was so good that the fast freight usually was loaded full both ways each trip. Johnny Wolfley supposedly made record time by driving his stage from Visalia to Smith House in exactly seven hours and 40 minutes.

The centers of activity had not changed much since the earlier boom days. Smith House still was the middle of town. There the stages, mail, whiskey, and the people all arrived. There the best dinners were served, the best dances were held, and the best news and gossip were related. Ford's Camp was popular too, and so were the assay offices. From the sheer numbers of people with a need for lumber, Weishar's saw mill down the road was always full of activity. Dog Town too, was a busy place. It had been Harry's Bend, then it was called Sunny Slope, but in 1879 the biggest butcher shop in the valley was set up there and the dogs gathered around it as much as the people did. So Harry's Bend became Dog Town.

There was much to talk about at the gatherings. On September 3 elections were held for the first set of state and county officers under the new constitution. The mining district went Democratic. On September 6 the first mining accident occurred. Joseph Johnston and T. A. Dallas were injured by a dynamite blast in the McGinnis shaft. Johnston had one arm blown off. On September 8 a barn burned to the ground and John Crowley's buckboard burned with it.

There were dances at Smith House and Kelley's Hotel, and women coming in on the stage to attend them. There were mining men with Fowler, and some came on their own. A bridge down the road burned and a new one had to be built. On September 18 a rich strike was made on the "Big Jim." On September 30 a new stamp mill was contracted for on Doherty's place to be running in thirty days. The progress of the tramway was watched and discussed. On October 23 the wire cable came in and most of the camp went up the mountain to watch it being strung.

There was as much liquor as there had been in 1874, as many fights and brawls. On September 22 Arthur Crowley lamented in his dairy, ". . . nothing new today except plenty of drunks in town—8 or 10 discharged from the mill site because they wouldn't work yesterday." And the next day, ". . . Very quiet today except some drunk fellows who make a great deal of fuss about nothing."

Even so, the camp was respectable. There were some more families now, more stable business men involved, and the religious frontiersman still had his influence. Preachers gave sermons every Sunday and often, the young men stayed up all Saturday night dancing and drinking and then went directly to the Sunday preaching. There was even a full time physician, Dr. T. F. Pegg.

But if there was religion and order, there was prejudice too. In 1874 W. H. H. Hart of the New England Company had used Chinese labor to build his roads and his trails and to dig his tunnels. Now, five years later, California was in the middle of a "Chinese problem." It was there in 1874, too, but it had not yet developed into the issue that it became in the late 1870s.

The Chinese accumulated fast in California, reaching 25,000 by 1852—one out of ten people in the population. In the gold fields, the ratio was three out of ten, and a natural pattern of discrimination was begun. The Chinese worked for low wages, seemed content with a low standard of living, were clannish and different, not only in their color, but also in their language, dress and customs. They were a race apart, and the miners feared and distrusted them.

[49]

*Original butcher shop of Beulah, situated at Harry's Bend, create the designation of the old camp as "Dog Town."*

Before long, a state tax was levied against all foreign miners. A head tax of $50 was imposed upon immigrants not eligible for citizenship. Shipmasters and owners had to give bond that persons brought into the state would not likely become public charges or prostitutes. Another law imposed penalties for the renting of lodgings with less than 500 cubic feet of air space for each resident, and of course, the Chinese lived in far more crowded quarters than that. The Queue Ordinance was re-enacted requiring every prisoner committed to a county jail to have his hair cut within an inch of his scalp.

By 1873 most of these state laws had been found unconstitutional by the federal government. Although the local people of Visalia and Beulah may not have been happy with having the Chinese laborers brought in by the New England Tunnel and Smelting Company, they did not have a strong basis for objection.

By 1879, however, opposition to the Chinese had grown bitter. California's economy was depressed and the presence of alien, cheap labor created a furor. The constitutional convention in Sacramento acted. An anti-Chinese article was adopted. It protected the state from aliens who might prove "dangerous or detrimental." It prohibited employment of Chinese by corporations or on public works. It outlawed Asiatic coolieism as slavery, authorizing measures to prevent further immigration and to deal with those already in the state.

Federal judges quickly ruled against the article, but the people of the state took the matter into their own hands. They went with their demands to Washington and President Hayes sent a commission to China to negotiate a treaty, to regulate, limit or suspend the entrance or residence of Chinese laborers in the United States. The people went further than that. There were pogroms and killings, fires in Chinese laundries and houses, looting of stores, threats and demands. When J. W. Crowley started his toll road into Mineral King, he could never have thought of employing Chinese labor. Indians, perhaps, but never Chinese.

There were three brave people in the valley that year, however, and Arthur Crowley told their stories. "One day Tom Harris, who was running a saddle train carrying passengers to the mines before the road was opened, had two Chinamen aboard bound for the camp to start a wash house. There were nearly a hundred men at work on the steep River Hill. The boys waited until the Chinamen were about half way up the hill and in the midst of the men when one man asked them where they were going. They said, 'Me go Minnie King, makie wash house.' One of the men grabbed the bridle reins and told one Chinaman to turn around and go back. He said, 'No, me go Minnie King.' and at this part of the game one of the white men said, 'Come on boys, let's hang them.' Then the Chinaman said, 'Oh no, me go Visalia.'

"His horse was turned down hill. One of the boys hit the horse with a shovel and down the mountain they both went, hanging on to the horns of the saddles and most every man they passed hit the horses with their shovels. How they hung on to the saddles is a mystery, but I guess they got back to Visalia and Mineral King had no wash house.

"At another time the same year J. C. Hoy, proprietor of a hotel in Mineral King, went to Visalia for a Chinese cook. He arrived on the stage about six o'clock. The miners got wind of it and called a meeting and told Hoy they would allow no Chinese in Mineral King. He got quite 'het up,' and said he would keep the Chinaman if he had to use force. The miners then informed him that if the Chinaman did not leave camp on the next morning stage they would hang him and the Chinaman. After thinking the matter over he told the Chinaman to board the stage next morning, so a hanging bee was averted." Thus ended the Chinese problem in Mineral King.

The miners and families of Mineral King were a jealous people. Jealous of "their" valley, their unique community, their friendships with each other. What a man might be or might have been in the lower elevations was forgotten in Mineral King. Whoever took part or was allowed to take part in the great venture belonged. They were all of a kindred soul.

These were the days of silver toothpicks and mustache cups; of pistols and handguns; of ceramic dolls and gloves and hats; of sardine cans and tobacco tins; of gold pieces and silver dollars; of buckboards and wagons; of faith in the future more than in the past. There was drinking and some fighting, but in the evenings there were also friends gathered around small cabin fireplaces or at open campfires, talking of that faith in the future, dreaming of successes.

James Mankins remembered, "On Sundays, after a hearty meal of half cooked beans and perhaps a groundhog (a young one) stew, we would get together and discuss the assessments, chlorides, ruby silver and the probabilities of a smelter being put up."

There were dances and songfests, the talks of preachers and politicians, hunting and fishing, and quiet moments in the forests and alpine bowls above the valley.

Life was good in the year 1879.

# FIVE

---—◆—---

# THE DREAMERS

In the beginning, in America, there is always the Indian. Mineral King was no exception. It was a great White Indian Chief who led some of the first miners to the hidden valley. When Parole discovered it, he had a Paiute Indian with him. But the one Indian was a vision. And the other never returned. In fact, no Indian was ever seen or heard of again in the valley.

The central part of California was home to two very different kinds of Indians when the white man first came. There were the digger Indians who lived in great numbers in the Tulare and Buena Lake basins and in the sloughs of the Central Valley. They seldom traveled far, their greatest journeys made to trade with other tribes on the Pacific coast. They never went into the high Sierra. There was no need to go there. It was a fearful country to the digger, wild and unyielding and too difficult to climb. They never got higher than the lowest sections of the foothills.

But there were others who knew the great mountains and used them. The Patwishas, the Yokuts, the Monaches or Monos, the Yosemites, the Paiutes, and other tribes of the Central Sierra and eastern desert areas wandered the heights. They crossed the high passes and knew each other and were friends. They helped each other in their wars against the white man. They hunted and traded together in the mountains.

[53]

The Wuchchumni Indians on the western slopes made yearly trips in the summer months from their lower foothill villages up into the cool comfort of the higher forested sections. The tribe on the East Fork of the Kaweah River always moved its camp up into what is now the Atwell Mill-Silver City area. It was a good spot. The mountainsides were not too steep there, nor too thickly forested. Exposed granite boulders in which nature had eroded large solution pot holes were perfect for grinding acorn meal and for cooking their foods. An entire venison could be cooked at one time in some of the larger holes.

These Indians wandered the surrounding mountains and canyons on their hunting trips. They went to Hockett Meadow, they hunted in the White Chief Bowl. Evidence has been found of Indian campsites and hunting grounds along the valley floor. But, at some time before the arrival of the white man, the Mineral King Valley became tabu.

When Harry Parole and his Paiute companion first rode down into the Mineral King Valley, they found no Indian campsites. And the wild life had no fear of them. It seemed not to know man. Through the years Harry told his friends of that experience. Many of those who heard the story were disbelievers. To them, it was only another of Harry's tall yarns. Still, there was other evidence of some sort of tabu.

In 1879 when John W. Crowley contracted to build the toll road into Mineral King, he knew he could not use Chinese labor, so he expected to use at least some Indians. John was a friend of the Indian. From the time he had come to Tulare County there had been a mutual respect. The Indians worked for him and he hunted with them. A rancheria of one thousand Indians was only a quarter mile from his cattle ranch at Ash Spring. Others were just as close to his Cottage-Post Office Ranch. But there was never any trouble. The Indians worked well for him. They never stole. They trusted him and came to him with their problems and for his advice. He was given the name of "Big Eyes," and was treated with the respect of a chief.

John knew his Indian friends would do whatever he asked, and he knew that they needed money in that hard year of depression so he went to them. But the Indians would not work on the Mineral King road. They would go no farther up the East Fork Canyon than the area below the "Three Falls" above Silver City. They would not work on a road that led into that valley.

John Crowley never recorded that he found out why, what the tabu was; what disappointment, what terror came to fill the valley. But it was there, and for an unknown time until 1863 when Harry Parole disturbed its peace, the Mineral King Valley was probably one of the most primitive areas in the West.

The white man was a curious type. Never a man to be satisfied, never a person to covet his ease, he was a man whose photographs and tintypes show a strange cast to the eye. An expression of perhaps a little madness, perhaps a little genius. He was a man who could dare, a man who could believe, no matter what his fears and his failures and his shortcomings. He was a man of dreams and visions and adventures. He was a man who could work.

John Meadows was such a man. Meadows crossed the plains with his family in 1856 in a covered wagon. His daughter, Rhoda, was born on that trip. In the best tradition of wagon train adventures, John had an Indian tale to tell. When his baby girl was only three days old, an Indian came to their wagon, lifted the canvas, and grabbed Rhoda from her mother's arms. John Meadows heard the cries and ran to the rescue. He struck the Indian with his whip and his child was saved.

John settled his family near Visalia. When the Mineral King mining rush started, he was one of the forerunners. He built the first trail from the foothills into Beulah and he prospected and bought shares in several mines. It was said that he located some 60 claims in the valley. "John Meadows was the most enthusiastic and confident of the early locators," one of his contemporaries wrote, "rating his possessions worth a million dollars. He was a farmer, a stock-raiser, a miner, a preacher, and a fighter, but withal, a brave, honest and conscientious man."

Rhoda Meadows, saved by her father from the Indians, married Abe McGinnis. Abe was a man not unlike her father in his dreams and ambitions and his love of the mountains.

When Abe was 19, he left St. Louis for the new adventure of California. Going by way of the Isthmus of Panama, he contracted

[55]

*Empire Mountain as shown before trails and roads cut its surface. The Empire Mine was situated on the upper slopes of the peak. A tramway ran through the trees of the lower slopes to a mill at the base of the mountain.*

"Panama Fever" and landed in San Francisco in 1846, weak and with almost no money. He tried mining when gold was discovered, but it proved to be too hard on him, so he took what money he had and bought a store in Sacramento. There he was successful. But still, the call of adventure was strong. When Abe heard of the mining excitement of Mineral King, he decided to go. After 20 years in Sacramento, he pulled up stakes and made Beulah his home.

This time mining seemed to agree with Abe. He had interest in the Young America, the McGinnis Mine, the Lady Alice, and Half Potato Hill Mine. He married Rhoda Meadows, and they had five children. Minnie Kate was born in Mineral King. It was the

[56]

*The Empire lode, a vein of granite, limestone and gold bearing quartz high on Empire Mountain.*

family's only home at that time. During the winter months they would leave to stay with the Meadows in Visalia, but only as long as the snows made it absolutely necessary. Abe McGinnis was as permanent a citizen of the valley as the mining district ever had.

John Crowley was another man of dynamic energies. He first came to California in 1852 when he was 16, traveling the long journey by ship around Cape Horn. Then he went back home to Missouri by way of the Horn again. But he couldn't stay. The trail westward, the adventure called him. This time he went, as Abe McGinnis had, through the Isthmus of Panama. Then back again. Then overland across the emigrant trail two more times. Finally, in 1857 he married America Jane Clements and made the journey one more time to settle in Sonoma County in northern California.

Still he was restless. In 1862 he moved to Tulare County and there he tried to satisfy his energies with ranching and store keeping. But it was no good. In 1868 he sold his store with the idea of going to the Argentine Republic in South America. But America Jane delayed the trip when she became ill, and the plans were dropped altogether when she died.

In 1870 he married again and he and his oldest son and his new wife made their first trip into the Mineral King Valley to Harry's Bend. John may not have known that day what the valley would mean to him. It was to give him the adventure and excitement he needed. He would not need to move again. He stayed in Visalia trying every business he could find but Mineral King became his dream. He built its first road, he prospected, he poured thousands of dollars into the mines. In exchange for shares, he took over the presidency of the Toll Road Company and did the work of incorporating several of the mining companies. He set up an assay office in the valley. He even helped split shakes for the buildings that were rising.

The Barton brothers were such a part of the mining era of Mineral King that it would seem impossible that the boom could have existed without them. They and their father, James Barton, were there from 1873 on. In November 1873 Orlando went into Mineral King with a party of six men over Pleasant Work's trail, while Stephen went in by way of the Lovelace Milk Ranch. In 1874 Enos waited out the spring thaw at Silver City along with John Meadows and his trail crew, then he and Bill Thayer built the first cabin in the valley, shoveling away the snow to lay the rock foundations.

James Barton made several claims in the first rush of 1874. Enos and Orlando worked in the New England Company's smelter and ran a sawmill and prospected too. Jason teamed on the Mineral King road. Stephen was said to be one of the most respected men in the lore of mining in the district.

W. B. Wallace was a friend of Orlando's. They prospected together and ate beans and groundhog stew together and swapped their yarns. "Orlando is a true philosopher," Bill Wallace wrote. "An observer and thinker, and also the wielder of a facile pen. He not only looks at things, but he sees things. He looks into the soul of things. He is a good talker but a quiet one—never torrential. If he has occasion to swear he does so in a subdued tone which manifests surprise and habit rather than irritation. He acts on the principle that when one has nothing to say he should not exert himself to say it. He is impressed with the value of the motto, 'Blessed are they that expect nothing for they shall not be disappointed.'"

There were hundreds of other miners with their own dreams and expectations. Hundreds who wandered the valley's granite walls and made their "coyote hole" diggings.

James Mankins first joined the rush of 1874. He took his wife and two babies to spend the summer in Beulah, and joined Abe McGinnis one day in discovering the Mankins and McGinnis mines. On other days, he found the Carelode, Springlode, Sam Patch, Red Comanche, and several others of the coyote hole variety. Orlando Barton thought that Mankins probably discovered more good ore than anybody else in the district. "Oh, we were all very rich," Orlando wrote. "Oh, yes. We were all bonanza kings."

Wiley Watson was one of the oldest of the early prospectors. In his sixties, what could he hope to gain, what future was there for him to dream of? But as soon as he heard of the strike, Uncle Wiley packed up his belongings and went. He brought back to Visalia some ore samples and the decision that Visalia had better build a road into the valley before Porterville put one in over Farewell Gap. His interest in Mineral King went far beyond the scope of mining. He saw in it an area as rich in lumber resources and "sightseer" possibilities as it was in ore.

In 1874 Uncle Wiley came over Farewell Gap from the Little Kern with four trout in his coffee pot. Mineral King was filled with game, but there was not one fish. There were other fishless pockets in the Sierra, and just north of the Kings Canyon, the streams were barren more often than not. But the Kern and Little Kern were filled. Uncle Wiley turned his four fish into the Mineral King stream opposite Spring Creek, determineed that "his" valley would be lacking in nothing. Those four fish stocked the entire stream running west, and later, even most of the lakes in the Sawtooth Circle.

Harry Parole, Tom Fowler, the Crowleys, the Bartons, Wiley

Watson, almost everyone who made Mineral King his dream, thought of it as "his" valley. But there was no one who wrote more about his valley and his faith in it than Judge W. B. Wallace.

Bill Wallace came to the Sierra in 1874 to try to cure a hacking cough, and the high country became a way of life for him. It did cure his cough, and also his "brain-fag" and his tired soul. Every summer, he took time out from his work and disappeared from Visalia only to return in a few weeks with pen in hand to write article after article, column after column, about all the wonders he had seen and felt, to convince his fellow man: "There is but one way to get full value out of a vacation and that is for one to detach himself entirely from his usual mode of life, its business, its cares and its responsibilities; to get out of the routine of ordinary existence, to view new and dissimilar scenes, to see new faces, to find new companions, to think and talk along new lines.

"The home labors of us who are towndwellers and office workers are but little varied. We work in circles and move in grooves. We become slaves to petty habits. We rush to dinner and rush back to work. If the evening paper is delayed we are annoyed. If after an exceptionally fine meal no toothpick is at hand the face value of the meal is immediately discounted. For the evenings we grow to like slippered ease and lounging chairs and idle or quite amusements, and our muscles accustomed to but a limited degree of contraction and expansion, become weak and flaccid.

"I prefer the high mountains with their great spaces and extensive outlooks, their forests, matchless flower decked meadows, crystal lakes, trout streams and noiseless nooks, where one may rest or rustle as he wills."

Bill Wallace had lived in the gold counties of northern California and the excitement of the Mineral King Valley's promise caught him. He went to Mineral King and he roamed the hillsides and canyons as hundreds of other men did. He prospected, collected ore samples, and bought mine shares. He dreamed and believed in "his" valley as hundreds of other men did.

But if the other hundreds of men saw the rivers and the flowers and the animals and moments of solitude as Bill Wallace saw them, they did not record it. His was the pen that first told the outside world that Mineral King was more than mining, that the Sierra was

[60]

more than just a mountain barrier. He wrote of his love and his joys, and people came to see them and decided to come again.

W. O. Clough was a believer. Eccentric, loved and laughed at, friend and buffoon, teller of tall tales and the subject of more, he worked the mines of Mineral King longer than anyone else. There was much that Bill believed in. His long hair and flowing beard, like Sampson's, was the source of his strength. The wisdom of the animal world surpassed any of man's. The immortality of his own soul was a fact beyond question. Bill Clough would never die. And the valley of Mineral King would one day make his fortune.

Bill had his own religion and it was the driving force of his life. He did not swear, but on occasion he would drink. He would not cut his hair, but he kept it trimmed. He dressed in clothes typical of the picture of the old prospector, but on Sundays he wore his best; coat and trousers with suspenders, a white shirt, a derby hat, and fancy high-laced boots. He even combed and curled his beard. And under that fancy beard, hidden but most important, was a red bow tie. All the children in the valley had seen it. They were Mr. Clough's friends. He always had a smile for them, a story to tell about the animals who could talk to him, a secret place for them to explore.

He was loved not only by the children. There were many in camp who called him friend. But his religious convictions were a source of amusement to some of the prospectors. One of the favorite forms of entertainment for visitors to Mineral King were the campfires at which Bill Clough was asked to preach.

Bill loved to preach. He denounced the miners and the teamsters and the devil for their wicked ways. He cried because only the children and the animals were innocent. One of the miners would give Bill a drink on the side, and the devil grew larger, Bill's sermons more eloquent. Laughter would rise from the circle of men, and heckling would begin. Someone would say the whole affair was sacrilegious, but no one would leave.

Once while Bill was into the full fire of a sermon, someone set his coat tails on fire. Another time while he was preaching from a wagon, the brakes were slipped and old Bill flew on a wild ride down the hill. But the next day, he could go to the children and forget the wickedness of men. Or he could go off to roam the mountainsides,

[61]

W. O. Clough in his Sunday best; preacher, prospector, wanderer,
full time resident of Mineral King for many years.

certain in the knowledge that somewhere beneath his feet there was his fortune just waiting to be found.

Of all the characters who called Mineral King their home, none had changed their lives as much as had Harry and Mary Trauger. J. H. Trauger had been a miner at Leesburg, Idaho, and had been respected and successful enough to be elected in 1872 to the Idaho House of Representatives. When Mary was a girl, she had been the playmate of William McKinley who was later to become President of the United States. But when the Traugers appeared on the East Fork of the Kaweah in 1873, they had nothing. They settled on a small holding beyond Red Hill, known as the Bear Ranch. Later they built another home, the Last Chance, up the road to Mineral King between Lookout and Redwood Canyon.

There were conflicting stories as to why they had come out from Ohio. Some people said it was because Harry had become addicted to drink and had lost everything. Others said they had moved to San Jose, had lived in a plush mansion there, then had lost everything through stock gambling. Still others said that Mary had contracted tuberculosis and Harry had given up everything to bring her west to the open and rugged outdoor life to cure her.

Whatever their reason for coming, their life was rugged and simple. In short, they lived in poverty. Mary had her pictures taken in fine dresses that she had saved, but she made her work day clothes from large burlap bags, and some of them were works of art.

When the first mining rush started in 1873, the Traugers followed the miners into Beulah. Harry became superintendent of the New England Tunnel and Smelting Company. Mary became "angel" of the camp. Wherever there was trouble or need, little Mary was there.

When Arthur Crowley and his sister, brother, and two teachers went into Beulah in 1874 to spend the summer, he wrote an account of the trip up. They had gone with a pack train of about 15 animals, and Bert Smith was their packer and guide. "It was (at Mule Creek) I first met Mary Trauger," he wrote. "She and her husband Harry were camped there. She was alone when we arrived and as I turned a point, she was standing in the trail, and yelled out

*Mary Trauger, "angel" of Mineral King, 1889; dressed in clothes she saved for pictures.*

to me, 'Where is old Bert?' She had my sister and Miss Logan sleep in her tent that night. The next morning, July 4th, we packed up and started for our destination.

"Just as we were ready to start, Mrs. Trauger yelled at Bert and said she would go to Mineral King with us if he would let her ride one of the pack mules and he said to jump aboard if you can ride on top of one of the packs, which she did. As we rode up to the boarding house of the New England Tunnel and Smelting Co. the first thing we saw of mining life was two men engaged in a fist fight. Mrs. Trauger got off the pack and knowing both of the old sourdoughs very well, she yelled at them to stay with it. When one had the best of the fight she would bet on him, and when the other one seemed to be gaining ground she would say, 'Oh, I bet on him.' She was a friend of everyone."

The Traugers spent winter of 1878 in Mineral King along with the other employees of the ailing New England Company. Mary was the only woman to spend an entire winter in the valley during the silver rush days. When the snowslide in March struck the camp, she was there beside her husband, searching for buried men. They found one man when she heard a clock ticking beneath the snow.

That night Mary administered to the injured and comforted the frightened. There were many other times throughout her years in the valley and on the road when she was to do the same. When anyone became sick, Mary was there. She had known sickness herself. The story was told that when she had come to the mountains, she had been hemorrhaging and was so weak she could barely walk. Now she could ride a pack mule and it was a common sight to see Mary Trauger walking the 12 miles from their Last Chance Ranch to Mineral King in one day, to help someone else.

Harry Trauger was prospector, miner, road worker, rancher and permanent resident of the mining district during the days of the mighty Empire. Mary Trauger was nurse and friend of all, the Angel of Mineral King.

*Ten stamp quartz mill typical of the Empire mill, purchased by Tom Fowler in Grass Valley, California.*

# SIX

————◆————

# DREAMS DESTROYED

Snow had fallen before Arthur Crowley went down the hill to Visalia in October 1879. It continued to fall that winter as heavily as it had in 1878. Trouble began to fall too, quietly at first, hidden behind the brighter signs of success. Work crews were staying in Mineral King over the winter. They were working on the Empire and finishing construction of the stamp mill, and to all outside appearances everything seemed to be going well.

Tom Fowler was up and down the Mineral King road, going to Visalia, to San Francisco, bringing mining men and investors back with him. On December 4 the quartz mill began operations. On the evening of February 4, 1880, the first shipment of bullion made from the Empire Mine was brought down from Mineral King to Visalia. At last the Empire was no longer a dream. It was becoming a reality.

Then the storms came. It rained in Visalia and it rained more. From February 10, on through March and into April, the storms rolled in one after another. By April 6 Visalia had received over ten inches of rain for the season. And still it continued. April 12, 13, 14, 15. On the 16th Arthur Crowley wrote in his diary, ". . . rained again all last night and is stormy today—grain and grass is growing fast and prospects were never more flattering for Tulare County than this season."

But the rain in Visalia was snow at the Empire Mine. On that night of April 16, all the dreams were crushed. "Snowslide at Empire Mine," Arthur Crowley's diary recorded the next day. ". . . last night at 11 o'clock, so reports say, crushing lodging house and wounding four and 15 are missing at last report. . ."

It had come slowly but it ended quickly. An avalanche roared down the slopes of Empire Mountain and engulfed the buildings beside the mine. The experience was terrifying. The whole side of the mountain seemed to give way and crashed down into the Empire bunkhouse. There were 20 men sleeping inside when it was suddenly swept down the mountainside and demolished. Four of the men were badly injured.

The others scrambled their way out of the snow and destruction to help those who were trapped. Their clothes were lost, the pay they had received just the day before was buried. There was no shelter left for them to go to, no way to get the injured down the mountain.

They waited for daylight. Huddled in the snow, their hands and feet began to freeze. A few struggled in the darkness of the stormy night to reach the blacksmith shop. They built a fire in the forge and waited for daylight there.

The next morning, the Mineral King Valley received news of what had happened on the Empire. A rescue party was formed and a messenger was sent through the storm down to Visalia. The injured men and the frozen miners with frostbitten fingers and toes were sewn into bed ticks and dragged down the mountainside to camp. There they waited for help.

It came the next day. A little over 23 hours after a messenger had ridden into Visalia to cry the news of the disaster, a doctor with medical supplies, and three other men, made their way through the last four miles of snow on foot, and were at the bedsides of the injured miners.

Only one life was lost, and that was the life of the Empire Mine. The snowslide was the final blow. All through that winter there had been reports that the ore was coming out of the mine in quantity and that it was beautiful. But Tom Fowler had not been paying his bills. All the trips to San Francisco and to Mineral King and to San Francisco again were only the desperate moves of men who were watching a dream die.

Tom continued to pour his money and his hopes into the operation of the mine and to ask his creditors for a little more indulgence. Letters began to come in asking for payment. Mark Lavelle demanded that the mill, which had been placed on his claim without written permission, be turned over to him.

Tom Fowler grew impatient. His assets ran in the millions, he was an important and respected man. Suddenly, just because he was a little short on cash and the Empire ore was a little "rebellious" and slow to be worked, his enemies were trying to destroy him. But he would not give up the mine.

Walter M. Hawley of San Francisco was one of the principle creditors and he brought suit against Fowler. On February 17, 1880, just two weeks after the first shipment of bullion, the Empire's assets were attached. But still, Tom would not give up his mine. Hawley was made trustee of the Fowler estate and was to pay the debts and manage all of Fowler's holdings so the operation of the mine could continue.

By the time the snowslide struck, it looked like everything was under control. Lavelle had taken his claim for the mill to court, but it was still operating successfully. The ore continued to come out of the mine. The ailing Toll Road company had boosted its financing by levying a $10 assessment on its stock. Walter Hawley was made president of the Empire Mining Corporation and he was as eager to get his money back from it as Fowler was.

Then came the tragedy. The bunkhouse was gone, the tramway supports damaged or destroyed. The mill had to be closed without the supply of ore coming to it. The men had to be moved out of Mineral King because of the threat of more avalanches.

Still Fowler, and now Hawley, were not to be stopped. When the spring thaws came, Hawley had an investigation made of the Empire and the report was all good. The potential was still there. It only needed more work. Hawley and Fowler decided to make repairs and improve the mill. A five cent per share assessment was made on the Empire stock holders to gain money for the repairs. Operations began again.

[69]

*Arthur Crowley, 1881; son of John Crowley and developer of Mineral King as a summer resort.*

The other miners and prospectors hurried back to the mountains and by late July, the community was as busy as it had been the year before. On Wednesday, July 28, the revamped Empire Mill started operations again. On Thursday, August 5, Thomas Fowler rode down from his mountain with a bar of bullion from the Empire Mill.

Tom rode into Visalia on the Mineral King Express with his usual flourish. Here was the final proof, a bar of silver from the Empire Mine. He put the 105 pound brick of silver on display and invited his creditors to view it. They did. They found it had a high content of lead and they were not impressed. More suits were filed.

Desperate, Tom decided what Bevins of the New England Tunnel and Smelting Company had decided six years earlier. The rebellious ore needed to go through a roasting process for reduction. But Hawley was discouraged now and angry. He would authorize no more expenditures.

Fowler became angry in return. Hawley had not settled all his debts and Tom was still being plagued with law suits. He did not like Hawley's handling of his ranch affairs, and now Hawley refused to go on with the Empire Mine. That was going one step too far. Tom Fowler brought a suit of his own against Walter M. Hawley. Hawley countersued, but while litigations were being contested, Fowler regained some control of his lands. Immediately, he began looking for new backing, for more money to put into his mine.

But summer of 1880 had passed. The miners and prospectors had left, discouraged by the Empire's lack of success and by their own failures. By October almost no one was in camp, and that winter the valley was left undisturbed to gather her snows in peace.

In 1881 Tom tried again. He searched for new monies; he sent a few men up to work the Empire. He and Crabtree and Belden reorganized the White Chief Gold and Silver Mining Company and announced immediate operations on it. But nothing happened. Still no one came.

The stage made its last run in June. Smith House was the only hotel in operation. Almost the only people in the valley were the summer families who were beginning to make Mineral King their vacation home. Other regulars did not come. There was too much discouragement in the valley. If the mining was an increasing failure, the snowslides were even worse. They were becoming a constant threat.

In February, Clark Moore, George Smith, and another man had been working the White Chief Mine. When the snows reached 18 feet, they decided they had better leave until summer. The three started out on snowshoes, worried about a possible snowslide. They stayed about 50 yards apart from each other to try to prevent one. But it came. All three were swept to the bottom of the canyon near Spring Creek. Clark Moore and the other man survived. George Smith was buried. They found him in April, snow shoes sticking out of the snow.

Disaster had become a part of Mineral King mining. No longer was it a beautiful dream. Even Arthur Crowley, who had vowed that the valley would make his fortune, did not return that year. And summer of 1882 was no better. Tom Fowler made another half hearted attempt to open the mines, but no one responded.

"Where are they all?" Bill Wallace asked. "The exultant mine owner who walked the earth with head erect and heart elate, where is he? Where are the dreamers, the rainbow chasers of those early years? Where is the man of mighty projects, of magnificent schemes? Where is the penniless promoter, the impecunious builder of smelters and constructor of Sutro tunnels—the man who knew best how to do it with the money of others? Where is the chronicler of lost mines? Where is the grubstake prospector who with a burro load of supplies was ever ready to find hidden veins of wealth? Where is the mineralogist and the cyanide process man at whose magic touch the most rebellious ores would yield up their gold and silver? Where are the burly, stalwart men who drilled holes in granite?

"Where are the merry throngs of young men and women who danced the evenings away in the big dining room of the boarding house? Where are the clergymen miners who mixed preaching with prospecting? Where is the flotsam and jetsam, the human driftwood that idled about the camp, useless in any place or capacity; simply living, eating, dying.

"The body of one of these old-timers outlived his mind and he died in the Stockton insane asylum—the venerable Dr. George at the age of nearly 90 years quit prospecting on this solid earth. Gone

[72]

is the little one-eyed Cornishman who carried the mail a-foot into Mineral King in 1877. Gone too is the pacific and amourous Hibernian who nightly emptied his heart through his voice and woed an amiable and willing widow with the song of another Irishman . . ."

Tom Fowler left Mineral King and tried to gather his life back together again. In desperate financial trouble, he tried politics again, first in an attempt for the seat of lieutenant governor, then for state railway commissioner. He became chairman of a committee of settlers at Mussel Slough which was fighting the railroad's high taxes on their land. But failure met him at every turn. There was only his ranching left, and there was not even enough money for that. He went to Mexico for a time, on business it was stated. He returned, still penniless and ill, the victim some had heard of several heart attacks or strokes. Others had heard it was of drinking.

In April 1884 the man who had been everybody's friend went to San Francisco in a final attempt to secure help from old friends. He wrote a deposition there, taken at the Grand Hotel. It was the final act of a man who had dreamed and dared and had lost. "I am in litigation now with Mr. Walter M. Hawley," he recorded, "of the firm of Marcus C. Hawley and others, in fact, with almost everybody that I owed anything to."

There was no hope. The Honorable Thomas Fowler returned home on the railroad he was fighting. As he stepped off the train at Goshen he fell. Bruised and sick, he died the next night in Visalia.

Big John Meadows died as he had lived, a part of the western frontier. In 1881 he took his wife and several children and stock into the Tonto Basin in Arizona. In July of that year the White Mountain Apache Indians went on the warpath there, and this time John could not use a whip in defense. He and his wife and one son, Henry, were killed.

When once again mining was a failure for Abe McGinnis, he took his family down to the Central Valley from Mineral King. He settled there and raised stock, had a slaughter house, and lived a quiet and ordered life. He died quietly in 1879, Rhoda in 1909.

John Crowley had put time and labor and money into his

[73]

dreams. He had taxed every energy he had. In December of 1881, exhausted and ill, he refused to leave his busy store in Visalia. Two days later he was dead. At the age of 45, he had done enough and lived enough for two lifetimes.

James Mankins' dreams were never realized either, and still he could say years later, "When I think of those days and those dear old boys I seem to choke. I feel like saying, 'Come back, boys', but no, I am selfish. They cannot come back."

Orlando Barton became an old gentleman with many memories, his children and his brothers' children and their children staying on in Mineral King as summer families.

Mineral King became a summer retreat for Bill Wallace, too. When the mining failed, the valley was still just as beautiful to him. In 1898 he was appointed a superior court judge in Tulare County, but that did not change his way of life. He still went up to his mountains, and he never gave up his hopes. The price of silver had declined, the Mineral King ores had proven too difficult to extract profitably, disaster had plagued every venture, but Bill Wallace still could look at the positive side.

In his opinion, the assays showed high enough to bring a good profit even with the decline in value of silver. New methods of mining and reducing ores were lowering expenses and making it possible to mine difficult veins that had previously been thought impossible. No one had seriously tried to work or market the copper and lead that filled the lower portions of the valley. Someone told Bill that the presence of zinc was no longer a serious impediment to the successful working of silver ores.

"To conclude," he wrote in 1905, "I make this broad statement: No mine in Mineral King has been developed or extensively prospected. All efforts made there to work the ores have failed either through ignorance or design . . . If that district were in some remote, rainless and treeless region, instead of being where water and timber and most of the necessary fluxes for smelting are at hand, in abundance, and within forty miles of a railroad, experienced miners by the score would be prospecting its ridges and canyons." Judge W. B. Wallace was a believer.

Bill Clough not only believed, he refused to give up. After the failure of Fowler's mine, he still roamed the mountainsides pros-

*Emma Gilliam Crowley; Arthur's wife and helpmate in the running of the resort.*

pecting on his own, working assessments for other people's claims. In 1885, while he was on a prospecting trip outside the Mineral King Valley, he discovered a vast cave. He took his friends to see it and it became a favorite attraction to the people of the San Joaquin Valley. They came to Clough's Cave and took out souvenirs of stalactites and stalagmites. Finally the Forest Service and then the Park Service closed the cave, and for years it was off limits to the public while the cave formations had a chance to rebuild. Now Clough's Cave is one of the tourist attractions in Sequoia National Park.

In 1896 the Empire Mine became Bill's property. He did the required work on it, driving the tunnel in to 800 feet. Every year when the summer families had gone down to the Central Valley, old Bill would pack his burro, go up to the Empire Mine to do his assessment work, then he would go off to relocate claims for some of his friends. After the first of the year, he would make his way through the snows to Visalia to file all the claims for himself and his friends as then required by law.

In February 1909 the Visalia *Times Delta* ran an article on the return of Bill Clough from the mountains. "Three weeks ago Mr. Clough came down from the Empire Mine to Mineral King with the idea of coming out to the valley. He made the trip on skees. That night it began snowing and for three weeks he was unable to leave. . . . Asked how his food held out, Mr. Clough stated that he ran out of bacon about three weeks ago, but he had three kinds of dried fruit, flour, baking powder and plenty of beans and red peppers. 'Beans and red peppers make the finest soup in the world,' he added. Mr. Clough keeps track of the days by making a dot, as he says, every time he works a day. This year he made two too many dots, and thought it was Washington's Birthday when he reached Three Rivers last Saturday.

"Mr. Clough states that he uncovered some fine bodies of ore this year, and he has some rich looking samples with him. In about a week he will go to Los Angeles, with the intention of disposing of some of his claims, and if he cannot do this he will organize a stock company, and ship out the ore himself. He states that it is all high grade stuff, and that there is enough there to make a great many big fortunes."

[76]

As Bill grew older he worked the mines a little less, but he still worked them. He grew even stronger in his religious faith and became a follower of the House of David sect of Benton Harbor, Michigan. He took odd jobs around Mineral King in the summer. In the fall before coming "out of the hills" to Visalia, he closed the power company dams that had been built at the lakes above the valley. Then in the winter of 1917-1918 Bill did not come down from the hills at all.

Years later a skull, a few pieces of bone, a weathered shoe, and what some believed to be the remains of a white beard, were found beside the trail to Franklin Lake. A short time later, a sign was nailed to a tree marking the spot where Bill Clough had died.

But there were those who did not believe it. Mr. Clough himself had told them he would never die. And he was their friend. He could talk to the animals. He could even hide a red bow tie under his beard. That was immortality enough. That was greatness.

Throughout their productive years, the Traugers' lives never changed. Their holding between Lookout and Redwood Canyon became known as Trauger's, a favorite place for the teamsters to camp overnight. In 1884 the White Chief Mine and all other property of the New England Tunnel and Smelting Company was transferred to Harry for the express consideration of one hundred dollars. For years he worked on the mine, extending the tunnel, waiting for another developer to come his way. But nothing ever happened. Never relieved of their poverty, still the Traugers could give whatever they had to their friends and those in need. If there was not much food on the table, it could still be shared. Harry was the last recorder of the Mineral King Mining District, but it was a job without financial reward now. In all their years of working and mining in Mineral King, the Traugers had received nothing.

Still, there was one great moment to come in Mary's life. When William McKinley was elected President of the United States, Mary scraped up some money and on December 3, 1896, she traveled to Washington D.C. to see him. When the President saw her he hugged her and laughed, and they spent some moments recalling their childhood days together. It was worth all the scraping she had done, to have that memory.

[77]

The years passed and Mary and Harry finally left the mountains and moved into a modern bungalow in Los Angeles with ". . . 6 rooms and Bathroom and oh just got things so handy now can't find whare to put anything—has just lived in trunks and Boxes and sacks and bottles so longe I don't know how to behave."

It did not last long. Their son was killed in Alaska while on a mining venture there, and Harry died in 1919. Mary moved to Hemet. As she grew older and more disabled she depended more and more on the generosity of those whom she had helped, to aid her now. "I often think how strange to see myself now . . ." she wrote to Arthur Crowley in 1929. "I used to start from Last Chance and walk to Three Rivers and catch stage for town [Visalia], have a tooth pulled and stage it to Lemon Cove, then walk home.

"And not think bad for an old pluck like me in Mineral King to bake four loaves of bread in forenoon and load on Hassey and walk up to Empire Mine and get supper for Harry and Uncle Bill and Chris Buttemen and wash for the old batchlers, mend their duds, make soape and wash again.

"Well, such was life. We had not goten our 30 thousand for our mining property. So we had to do the best we could. We lived just the same. Our love for each other held us together."

And what of Harry O'Farrell? He had made his fortune, he had spent it. But he came back. He prospected, he roamed the Sierra, he hunted, he fished, he prospected more. He talked with his friends, ate with them, and was, as Orlando Barton said, "an oracle of wisdom" to them. He dreamed his own lonely dreams. One day he returned to his cabin at Harry's Bend and stood beside the doorway, looking out at his valley, up at his Empire Mountain. A few days later, no one had seen Harry. They went to look for him. He was still in his cabin, beside the open doorway. Harry Parole had died in his valley as he had lived, alone.

And all the other men and women, those whose names we do not know. They are in a dream. They are held immortal in the vision of a mighty Empire.

# SEVEN

---◆---

# THE DOLDRUMS

The world was not the same in 1882. Suddenly the old ways were changing. Life was moving faster, man's interests were being widened. The pioneer had settled, the westbound emigrant could go no farther. His children were grown and filling the land. California was no longer a wilderness.

Politics were growing big time. Some men's influence stretched from one end of the state to the other, even from one side of the nation to the other. California could let Washington City know what she wanted, and Washington City listened.

There was communication. From everywhere there was news. Day to day, flying cross country with the railroads, the word came. Through newspapers, Visalia and all the other small, isolated California towns knew what was happening.

On May 9 Arthur Crowley could record in his diary, "President Arthur signed the Chinese bill prohibiting them from coming to the U.S. for ten years." On June 30 "Charles Guiteau, the assassin of President Garfield, was hanged today at Washington City at 7:35 p.m." July 20, "Outbreak in Arizona with the White Mountain Apaches—John Meadows and family reported to be killed." And on July 22, "British making things hot for the Egyptians." California was a part of the world.

And Californians became interested in the world. The frontiers of their nation had been settled so they must look beyond their borders. Some went to Mexico, others on southward into Argentina where it had been common knowledge for years that if a man could endure a few hardships, he could become a cattle baron in no time at all. Some went to seek the gold wealth of Alaska or the new frontiers of the Canadian plains. Some even crossed the oceans, to South Africa, for the gold and diamonds and adventure there.


Those who remained and who were educated well enough, read the magazines and newspapers that brought the world to them. Suddenly there were new cultures and new people and new ideas. The industrial age was burgeoning. It seemed there was nothing that could not be invented once it was dreamed of. Within one decade there had come to the public market such wonders as imagination had hardly dared to admit a lifetime ago. The submarine, elevators, gasoline engines; English steam carriages, phosphorous "strike anywhere" matches, and the phonograph; sewing machines, washing machines, even the carpet sweeper. The miracle of the telephone in 1881 stretching long distance from city to city; refrigerated railway cars carrying pork to California from the mid-west; overseas mail service, overseas telegraph; at county fairs, balloons that rose into the sky carrying men into mere specks above and beyond the horizon.

The Electric Age dawned in 1882. Thomas Edison's first power plant went into operation in New York. Two years later the fountain pen and linotype were invented. A milk bottling machine was conceived in 1885, and a gasoline engine was put into an autocarriage, producing a kind of three wheeled motorcycle. And in 1888 the Kodak camera, the wonder that enabled anyone and everyone to take their own photos, was marketed. No more horse and carriage, the covered wagon, the clumsy ox drawn plow— "now behold the mighty gang plows," the *History of Tulare County* proclaimed in 1883, "yoked to a score of snorting steeds and cutting a broad swath of brown mold across the green prairie, from horizon to horizon. Next the automatic seeder scatters the germs by millions. Not the slow sickle, or puny scythe must reap the harvest. The swift headers come, with waving wings and rattling blades. And last—no wooden flail with feeble beat, nor old-time fanning mill, but the mighty steam separator, devouring heads by millions, and making immediate return in hundreds of tons of clean, bright grain."

In Visalia, the weekly shows in the Armory beckoned new talent. "Uncle Tom's Cabin" drew a large and enthusiastic crowd and the play was reported to be excellent, the acting worthy of San Francisco or even New York. There were constant shows, circuses, parades, fairs, concerts. Culture had come to California.

As if to welcome the brilliance of a new age, a large comet swept across the eastern sky. Between September 25 and October 16, 1882, it awakened the California morning.

Hard times left the state. The weather was favorable and business prospered. New schemes rose and developed. Irrigation of the desert lands; borax and petroleum prospecting; resorts for the wealthy and the idle, brought by the coming of the railroad and the California climate.

In 1883 Tulare County, blushing with the prospects of its great successes, published its own history. It had reached the mature age of 31, had 11,280 official residents within its boundaries, and it could take time now to look back at its "Early Times and Troubles" and to modestly predict that it was ". . . destined to eventually become one of the most prosperous and favored regions on the continent." It talked of the vast soil, mineral and agricultural resources that had barely been tapped. It devoted sections on mining, on Mineral King and the Empire Mine. "Fowler undertook the development of the Empire Mine that has proven so rich," the history stated. "The ore yields from one-tenth to one quarter gold. Ore has been taken out of the Silver Lake Mine paying $200 to $300 per ton."

Such words could have been enough to foretell another rush. But the exuberance, the excitement of the 1880s were passing Mineral King by. There were new, more promising ventures to look to. Now the old settlement of Beulah was merely a refuge from the Central Valley summer heat.

[81]

*Support tower for the Empire tramway built in 1879 by Andrew Hallidie, the originator of the San Francisco cable car system.*

There was not even much claim-filing done. From 1881 through 1883 the mighty Empire was filed on by A. G. Anderson. In 1884 and on through 1886 Harry Trauger took over the claim. Bill Clough filed on a few others, but not so much out of hope as out of habit. In the 1882 election only 23 votes were cast in the Mineral King District; 14 for Garfield, 8 for Hancock. Even as a retreat from the hot season in the San Joaquin, Sweet's Mill was a more popular place to go.

In August 1882 Arthur Crowley and some friends went up to Beulah and over to the Kern to camp and hunt and fish. But it was not the same as it had been in the old days. The fishing was good, the card playing with his hunting companions relaxing, the beauties of the area were still there. But the old friends in camp were missing, the dances and meetings and bonfires with preachers. And the hunting was terrible. "I am perfectly disgusted with hunting in these regions," Arthur wrote, and he and his companions packed up their gear and went home.

Even the History of Tulare County had to admit at the end of its section on Mineral King, ". . . The town or mining camp of Mineral King contains about fifty houses, including the Empire Stamp and Reduction Works. At present, it is in torpid condition."

The only activities of any note came in 1886. The Loup brothers, their faith in the valley's future undaunted, stocked Eagle Lake with about four hundred fish caught from the Mineral King stream. In the same year, A. J. Atwell, a retired judge from Visalia, decided to try the new recreation industry and a little lumbering as well. He bought Isham Mullenix's old mill and 140 acres of homesteaded land down the road from Mineral King. On it he built a new sawmill, with cabins and a campground for Valley visitors.

Arthur Crowley began to think of recreational possibilities, too. He joined with Judge Atwell in repairing the road up to Beulah so it would be passable for the summer families. But responsibilities took him away from whatever new dreams for Mineral King he might have. In 1885 Arthur married Emma Gilliam, the girl he had courted for seven years. In 1887 they moved to Los Angeles where he could support a family in style. Beulah was far away.

All in all, the 1880s were a time of rest for the Mineral King Valley. It was one small pocket of escape from the excitement of a world racing faster. The short, dark tunnels on the hillsides were silent and abandoned. The Empire equipment was still. Peace had returned; the valley could begin to mend her scars.

While Mineral King rested, the surrounding Southern Sierra lay besieged in a state of battle. Conservationists had discovered the Big Trees. The Giant Sequoia were being cut. Lumbermen were going into the Sierra north of Visalia and cutting out whole mountainsides. Since 1862 logging operations had been destroying them until the groves were only about one third their original size. The two largest trees in the world had already been felled. The Giant Forest, the greatest grove in the world, was being threatened. Even at Atwell's Mill below Mineral King some of the big trees were being cut.

The conservation movement was growing. Not only men such as Gifford Pinchot, John Muir and Stephen Mather were concerned now. For the first time, the general public saw something to preserve. "A man has not seen California until he has spent a week in the deep recesses of a redwood forest," the 1883 *History of Tulare County* told the world. "It is then, standing beside the towering monarch of the forest, that a man will realize his utter insignificance, and how inestimably ephemeral he is compared with many other of God's handiworks. He looks upon a tree that stood when Christ was yet in his youth, the circles of whose growth but mark the cycles of time almost since the first man was, and on whose tablets might have been written the records of mighty men of old."

The people were convinced. Finally Congress was convinced. On September 25, 1890, with President Harrison's signature, the giant tree was preserved, for all men, for all time. The Sequoia and General Grant National Parks were created. Pandora's box had been opened. Immediately California and the other Western states wanted more. It was with good reason. Not only were their timbered mountainlands falling fast to the saw, but fires were sweeping across them too, threatening even the lower range lands where people lived.

In this, the sheepherders were the villains. They roamed the mountain meadows and the hillsides in the summer, and in the fall

*The Honorable Thomas Fowler, rancher, California State Senator, and developer of the Empire Mine.*

*Catch of trout from Franklin Lake, 1882, just eight years after storekeeper Wiley Watson brought the first fish into Mineral King in a coffee pot.*

on their way to the lower valleys, they burned the ranges behind them so the grasses would grow more lush for the coming year. Unfortunately, not only the grasses burned, the forests did too. The sheepmen left the conflagrations behind them untended, satisfied that they would create more rangeland in the wake of their devastation.

In 1891, the Forest Reserves Act was passed and thousands of acres of western land were closed to any use. In California, the San Bernardino and Sierra Reserves were created. The Sierra Forest Reserve, formed in 1893, was immense. It covered more than three million acres in the southern and central Sierra Nevada. The valley of Mineral King was in its midst.

If Mineral King had fallen victim to the doldrums in the 1880s, the entire Sierra became torpid now. Not only were the sheepmen and lumbermen run off the mountains, no one else could make use of the lands either. The people of the San Joaquin Valley became alarmed. Within a period of three years, their mountains had been closed to them. They could go to the Giant Forest and stand in awe beneath its trees; but they could no longer graze their cattle in the meadows; they could not hunt along the wooded trails; they could not camp upon their own patented lands. They could go to Mineral King and spend the lazy weeks fishing and hiking; but they could not hunt there, either; they could not work their claims and mines; they could not even prospect legally.

And everywhere, there was the presence of the military. The first troops came from San Francisco in 1891 to guard the new Sequoia National Park. One unit camped at Cain's Flat below Atwell's Mill, but it did not restrict its presence to the Park lands. It moved up into the Mineral King Valley and camped near the Spring Creek outlet. It even had a parade ground there, and the area became known as "Soldier's Flat."

It was a high price the people had paid to save their forests. Perhaps higher than they had expected. There was grumbling. There were violations of the bans on hunting and grazing and prospecting. Sometimes there were clashes, verbal and physical, with the soldiers. But the fires in the forest were not such a threat now. New logging roads no longer scarred the land. And the people did go to see the big trees.

A time of quiet had come. Now not only Mineral King but the whole Sierra could mend her scars. It was a time she needed. Man had come too quickly and had taken too much.

*The Mineral King Resort in the 1880s*

# EIGHT

———————— ◀◆▶ ————————

# SUMMER REFUGE

With all the restrictions, Mineral King should have slept longer. Because of one man, it did not.

In 1872, when Arthur Crowley was a young boy of 14, he had vowed to make some part of the Mineral King Valley his. For years he invested in the mines, but there had been no return. Perhaps some day there would be. But now there was a new resource to be considered. That resource was tourism.

When the railroads swept across California, they brought a new industry. For the first time travel was convenient. No more bouncing wagons and dust and discomfort. Now, in a day it was possible to go places that would have taken several days before. People were not wasting the opportunity. Resorts were blossoming everywhere. To go, to see, to be idle, to be pampered, this was the new leisure.

The people of Visalia were joining the trend. Sequoia National Park, Sweet's Mill, even Judge Atwell's campground and cabins were growing popular.

Arthur Crowley saw his opportunity. He and his family had tried Los Angeles, but home and Mineral King called them back. In 1890 Arthur purchased the old "Smith House" hotel in Mineral King. It was not in the best condition now, but it was big and its location on the valley floor was the best. Next he filed two claims. On May 26 he relocated the Empire Number One, Extension North, first located by John Jordan on October 7, 1873, and filed his claim in the government books. Then on June 20 he located the Empire mill site and within its five acre boundaries just happened to rest the Smith House.

He could do no more that year. Depression had hit California. Interest rates soared, money was hard to come by, business was quiet everywhere. There was hunger and unemployment. There were diptheria and pneumonia epidemics. There were record snows in the mountains and there were record floods in the valleys. The excitement of the 1880s had hit a hard end. It was the beginning of troubled years.

Arthur Crowley could not afford to put money into Mineral King, but each year he did. He helped repair the road in the spring, each family along the road paying a share of the cost. In 1891 the county agreed to pay Arthur $100 for the job. It cost $200 for Harry Trauger to do the work, and the residents paid the extra cost again. The Park soldiers, newly arrived at Cain's Flat, helped for a few days. When they reached Mineral King in the middle of May, they found three feet of snow on the ground and six or eight cabins demolished by snowslides. Nothing was easy.

But the people were used to hard times in Mineral King. Whatever happened there during the winter, the coming of spring would erase. The stream would flow, the flowers would bloom, the deer would roam the meadows. Cabins could be raised again. Fallen timbers could be used for bonfires.

In July 1891 it was reported that not less than 200 people were in camp, escaping summer heat in the San Joaquin, escaping the hard times of the "gay nineties". On July 20 the *Tulare County Times* carried an article headed "Mineral King Notes." It told of some of the families in camp and of a social held around an evening campfire at which 75 people were present.

"Wm. Danielson of Visalia was elected mayor of the city by unanimous vote and he enforces his duties with due dignity and impartiality. Johnny Bell, generally known in camp as "toughey," is marshal of the camp. He left for Visalia soon after being elected to the distinguished position for the purpose of having a badge of office manufactured at a foundry or harness shop, with a promise to return to his duties on Friday next. The statement that he had entered into negotiations with (Sequoia National Park Superintendent) Captain Dorst for a detachment of soldiers to accompany him on his return to camp with his badge is indignantly denied.

"Lawyer Meux was arrested on Wednesday of last week on the charge of washing his feet in the headwaters of the Kaweah River and above the campground. He was taken before Judge Annie Mills Johnston and pleaded not guilty to the charge. Judge W. A. Gray appeared on the part of the prosecution while Mr. Meux acted as his own attorney. The case was tried before a jury of twelve ladies."

Arthur Crowley filed a proof of labor on his mine and mill site that summer and he settled his growing family in the Smith House. He worked on the road and on his claims. He fished and attended the socials, too.

In spring of 1895 work on the Mineral King road started again, but this time it required more than a job of patching. From March 20 until May 4, a crew of from 10 to 18 men worked on the rain washed roadway; such men as Harry Trauger, Bill Clough, Charley Blossom, the Atwoods, Harry O'Farrell, and Arthur Crowley. When it was finished, work was started on the Crowley resort. "We have got the upstairs (of the Smith House) partitioned off," Arthur wrote to his wife, Emma, on June 7. "Have got ten bedsteads up there, hope we can have them occupied all summer. We have got the Ford house nearly finished, and I tell you it is going to look nobby. We will go to work on the barn as soon as we finish the Ford house. . . . Make some enquiries about wool matrasses and other kinds, also pillows and blankets. I hardly think I will bring up any spring matrasses. I believe by having tick filled with straw, and wool matrass over it will be just as good and it will be a good deal cheaper."

The Smith House was converted to a luxury such as "Whiskey" Smith had not provided. There were even lace curtains hung in the windows. By 1906 the Crowley resort had on its five acres a two-story hotel, a store, butcher shop, stable, a canvas covered dance hall, and more than half a dozen "cottages," the Ford house, Watson cabin, Samstag and Post Office cabins, the Mickle and Bodden and Shake cabins, and the Bell house.

[91]

People started coming. Hopes to have ten new bedsteads occupied all summer were more than met. The resort could not keep up with the demand. In 1898 two dollars board and lodging were charged by the day; $10 by the week; $8 board and $2.50 lodging by the week; $40 board by the month; single meals fifty cents; single beds fifty cents; horse feed one dollar per night, barley extra.

Families came to the Ford and Bodden cabins. Freight wagons lumbered up the dusty road once again. In 1896 Henry Alles started running the stage. Arthur petitioned Washington for a post office. On May 10, 1897, the application was approved and the post office in Mineral King was created, with Arthur Crowley officially appointed its postmaster. In 1902 a telephone line was stretched from Cain's Flat to Mineral King and connected with the Sunset Telephone Company's line down in Three Rivers so that, as the construction orders read, ". . . one may talk to any point in the Valley."

In 1905 permission was granted by the Forest Service for a water pipe to be laid from Spring Creek to "camp" and gone were the problems of the past years when water had to be carried from the river to the hotel and store. Now there was clear water without mud and silt and contamination from dirty feet.

The camp was not the same as it had been in the 1870s. It had become a family resort. There were dances in the canvas covered hall and concerts by everyone who had any talents at all. There were picnics and watermelon feasts. There were bonfires and songfests. Mineral King became a way of life. Not only the summer regulars came now, but also people of greater renown. There were visitors from other states. A party of United States Congressmen came in over Timber Gap on tour of the Park and Reserve. John Muir passed through the valley one year.

But the regulars were no less interesting. There was Anna Mills Johnston, one of the first women to climb Mt. Whitney. There were lawyers who left their families in Mineral King while they went camping in the back country to "read law." There was Uncle Len Cutler, the handyman of the resort. There was still old Bill Clough, the Sunday bonfire preacher. And there were the members of the liar's club, who spent each night spinning yarns around the old pot-belly stove of the store. Eugene Paulette, who called himself Robert Edson in his motion picture roles; Bert Smith, one of the Mineral King packers and a stockman in the Valley; "Windy" Stevens, back country guide and packer; F. N. Eggers, expert black-jack player; "Uncle" Billie Course; Arthur Crowley; Bert Weisner; Dr. Bruce Montgomery; Bob Barton; and the greatest character and liar of them all, Benjamin Franklin Harris.

Ben Harris was an unlikely candidate for statewide renown. In his yarn-spinning days, he was a desperately crippled man who sometimes had to crawl through the dirt to reach his horse-drawn spring wagon. Once he had worked for a lumbering company and then became a packer and meat hunter for the first Mineral King mining rush. But throughout most of his healthy years he had roamed the mountain valleys alone, living off fish and deer and bear.

In his lame years he cared for himself still, accepting only a little food from his friends. He visited families of Visalia, Farmersville, Lemon Cove, and Dry Creek in the winter, entertaining them with his tales. In the summers he stayed in Mineral King, his wagon usually the first one up the road in the late spring. Ben was dirty and ragged, and the women of Visalia and Mineral King hesitated to invite him to their homes. But the children and men loved him.

In time, there were more Ben Harris stories than anyone could remember. Newspapers put them into their columns. *Fortnight Magazine* printed an article about him and his tales. Most of Ben's tall ones were unprintable. He was not a man of gentle words. But there were some favorites that were told to everyone year after year beside the old potbelly stove in the Mineral King store.

"See them antlers above the door there? Biggest antlers you'll ever find anywhere, I reckon. I ever tell you about where they come from? Got 'em on a huntin' trip few years back down on Rifle Creek. Old Bill and me, we seen some buck tracks up the ridge over toward Shotgun, there, and we started out for them. We went up the canyon and followed them tracks for a mile or so toward some cliffs there, then they petered out.

"Old Bill and me decided then we better split up, and he went on up the canyon and I circled on 'round the cliffs. All of a sudden I thought I heard something behind me, and by God, there he be. There was the biggest old seven pointer that ever set foot in these

*Atwell's Mill below Silver City, formerly Isham Mullenix's mill; the largest enduring lumber mill of the area, producing lumber for homes, mines and a redwood water flume.*

Sierras, a-followin' and a-sniffin' at my tracks. Soon as I turned he reared up his head and 'fore I knew it, he was hid behind a old, gnarled juniper tree with just his flanks a-showin'.'

"Now you can see I was up against it. To shoot into them flanks was to ruin the best venison ham ever found in the west. I sighted and found I just had room to hit his back bone between the tree and the right ham. Tight, but I knew I'd never get another chance. Well, by God, I never hit a bulls-eye cleaner than I hit that bit of back bone. He fell and it 'peared like he never had a spark of life left in him, but I crept up to rip open his throat just to make sure. He had fell with his head right under that juniper tree, so I sort of had to step over him to get to his throat.

"I just had the old dirk drawn and a second more would a done the work, when up he jumps with me on his back and a-headin' like blue blazes for the canyon. Now, I tell you, I couldn't jump off, he

*Grove of Giant Sequoias at Atwell's Mill, 1911; a subject of conservationists' concerns since the 1880s.*

was goin' that fast. Camp was two miles away, but I figured the only hope I had was in headin' there and maybe old Bill would be back there to stop us.

"You ever rode a deer? Well now, it ain't all it's cracked up to be. But still, if you keep a steady nerve and think twicet where he thinks oncet, you can come out a-winnin'. By real strategy, now, I kept that old buck headin' straight for camp. And just as I was thinkin' I couldn't hang on to them old trees of his no longer, I heard Bill a whoopin'. One more jump landed us right in the middle of camp and I lifted up my left leg just a little to give old Bill a place to shoot.

"Well, Bill's rifle did the rest. And say, boys, I'm tellin' you the truth now. I rode that buck for two miles clean into camp. And if you don't believe me, just look at the velvet from them horns that I ain't never been able to clean out'n my hands since.

"Now, I tell you, my bones was achin' some after that ride. But what made me most sore of all was what Bill done. You know what he done? After all that, old Bill, he had the guts to claim that deer for his'n. He took that deer and he put them antlers right there above that door!"

Hunting and fishing were always good for some tall tales. Game was still not as plentiful as it had been in the days before the mighty Empire. But hunting trips could be made to the back country of the Kern, and on occasion, the Superintendent of Sequoia National Park would issue a sixty day permit to hunt in the Park.

Almost every man had a full armory of weapons. Arthur Crowley's was typical: one 1856 .45 caliber rifle a "fine Damascus" 12-gauge shotgun; an 1886 .38 caliber self-cocking, black ivory handled pocket pistol; an 1879 .22 caliber Winchester repeating rifle; and an 1871 .44 caliber Colt Frontier six shooter.

If the hunting was not what it had been in years past, the fishing was much better. All the men in camp took an interest in the catches. They had stocked the streams and lakes themselves, and were still stocking them, sometimes keeping plantings a secret. From Wiley Watson's four trout brought over from the Little Kern in his coffee pot came the hundreds caught each summer. Arthur Crowley and Will Trauger stocked Mosquito Lake. The Loup brothers stocked Eagle. Arthur and Jeff Davis planted Silver. Nic Wren, Mark Lavelle and W. A. Ward planted Monarch. Arthur and his oldest daughter carried fish to Cliff Creek over Timber Gap and to the stream below the falls at the Gate and at Trauger's.

The fish that came out of the streams and lakes seemed to match the numbers being put in. It was not unusual to get 20 or 30, sometimes over 50 in a catch, with rainbow trout at least 12 or 15 inches long. In 1895 Arthur Crowley caught the first trout from Eagle Lake. There were five in the catch. The smallest was 29 inches long and the largest 36. After that, the big fish stories in camp began to grow.

There was always something in camp to do. Hunting and fishing were not the only pleasures. There were hikes to be taken, to the lakes and the gaps or to the springs and the different mines. Groups gathered to take evening walks, to the Gate or to Black Wolf Tunnel, to Spring Creek, to the Junipers at the head of the canyon. There were elderberries down at Atwell's Mill to be picked and made into jelly and wine. There was the Big Rock below Smith House for the children to climb.

There were willow horses to be ridden, skunk cabbage swords to be made for mock fights, and mud pies to be baked in the sun. When the stage came in, almost everyone in camp gathered at the store to wait for the mail and the milk. They all carried whatever containers they could find for the milk to be measured into from the huge demijohns in which they were delivered. On Sundays the young girls stood beside the sparking bench near the store flirting with soldiers from the park.

The years brought few changes. What differences there were, were mostly in the weather. In 1895 there were late snows and a profusion of wild flowers, and 1896 and 1897 were wet and beautiful, too. But the next three years were dry and hot with sand storms rising up from the San Joaquin even into Mineral King. The smoke and smell of timber fires filled the valley all summer long.

Still, whatever the seasons brought, there was always time. Time to rest, to see and feel, to know the valley and the mountains. There was time for lying in the meadows, watching the summer clouds form and dissolve in the sky. There was time for hearing jays and the tap of a woodpecker; the silence of the deep forest on a trail; the sound of the river rising at night, its gentle roar blending into sleep.

There was time to wait, to watch for the unusual, to notice the mountain phenomena; a lunar rainbow on the high cliffs above Juniper Ridge; balled lightning in Farewell Gap. Sometimes the evening had double shadows, the strong ones falling to the east as the sun set, faint ones to the west as the moon rose. On other evenings the twilight arch would cast the shadow of the earth upon the higher peaks. There was the perennial pattern of summer storms forming over Farewell Gap, the late fall and winter storms coming in over Timber Gap. In June the snow banks would turn red and pink.

It was small things that made Mineral King what it was. It was the sting of ice-coated water splashed on the face in the morning; the bitter shock of reaching into the "cold box" that sat in the stream below a cabin, to bring up milk or watermelon from its dark, icy depths. It was the feel of the mountain breeze, blowing up canyon in the day time, down canyon at night; and the sudden change in the valley's mood when the wind reversed, bringing a storm down the canyon with it. It was the warmth of the high altitude sunshine in a spot sheltered from the wind.

There was a sharpening of the senses by end of the summer, a sensitivity to the touch and feel of earth, to different odors of the valley; to the smell of empty sardine cans; to beans and coffee and campfires; to onions in a dinky stew. Bearbrush and pennyroyal, marshes and ants. Dirty towels and damp leather, the sweat of horses and dust. A bear close by. Wet willows by the stream. The smell of an approaching storm and the damp earth after it. The odor of a mountain morning with the pungence of pine needles and wood smoke from the stoves of the cabins.

Mineral King was still a dream. It was summers of endless feelings. It was the cling of wet trousers after a day of fishing. Soft dirt in your shoes on a hike. Walking across the flats on a carpet of "cat paws." The spongy softness of a wooded trail. It was the expanse of wilderness from a mountain peak, too vast for the eye or for the mind to comprehend. It was the excitement of a building thunderstorm. The gloom of a summer fog. The quiet of dusk as the surrounding peaks changed from red to gold to orange to red again, as the earth turned away from the sun. It was the quiet of the starlit nights. It was the quiet of a world at rest.

That was the beauty of the continuing summers. It was quiet. There was the eternal hope that mining might come to life again, that boom times might return. But it was difficult to imagine the valley any other way than what it was now. In 1897 it seemed it might change. The year before, the Secretary of Interior had asked the National Academy of Sciences to recommend a national forest policy, and in June 1897 the Academy's recommendations brought the passing by Congress of the Forest Reserves Act. Once again, the timbered mountain lands were open—open to lumbering, mining, settlement, prospecting.

It seemed all the old prospectors in Mineral King forgot why their mines had failed. Without government intervention, perhaps by now they would have realized their bonanza. Without the closing of the Reserves, perhaps a big company with new mining techniques might have come in.

Bill Wallace, Harry Trauger, Bob Laird, Bill Clough, Arthur Crowley, Samstag, the Davises, the Crabtrees, all rushed back to their mines. They relocated their claims and in the fall, the $50 assessment work began. They started looking for backing, in full confidence that with new mining processes, now the mines would be workable.

In 1898 they found their man. "Henry Harlow came in today to look at my Empire Mine," Arthur Crowley recorded with some excitement in his diary on August 12, 1898. And the next day, "I went up to the Empire in the forenoon with Harlow and got a lot of ore for him to take out—I offered him my Empire claim for $5000 cash down."

But the Empire was not the mine for the San Francisco promoter. He chose two others. On October 5 Arthur bought Bob Laird's half of the Chihuahua for $2,500 and bonded the mine to Harlow for $5,000, the bond to run for eight months. Then on December 5 Arthur and his brother Jim, along with Bill Wallace, bonded the Cherokee to Harlow for $7,500.

The excitement was running high. Henry Harlow contacted a firm of mining engineers in San Francisco concerning the operation

*Freight wagon and six horse team by the south side of Smith House; one or more freight wagons carried supplies from Smith House to Visalia each day during the mining era.*

of the mines. W. T. Farrar of the firm, said he would inspect the claims to see if he might be interested in taking them over.

The agony of waiting began. Winter came and snows closed the road. In the spring the miners worked their way into Mineral King to inspect their claims. By June 21 they sent word to Harlow that they were ready for the engineers. W. T. Farrar took his time. On July 3 he and two engineers finally arrived. They went up to the mines, quietly looked, took some samples, listened to the proposals for sale, and left camp without saying a word. On July 10 a letter arrived from Visalia. W. T. Farrar liked what he had seen, especially on Crowley's Chihuahua vein. He wanted to negotiate a bond but would wait until he reached San Francisco and has his samples assayed before he made a firm offer.

More waiting. Everyone was excited now. If the Chihuahua

proved workable, then so should many of the other mines. A month passed and there was no word from either Farrar or Harlow. On August 17 it finally came. "Dear Sir: Your favor of 16th rec'd in regard to your property at Mineral King . . . I took careful samples and the results were not satisfactory . . . when the location of the property is taken into consideration . . . the proposition is entirely a shipping one . . . the cost of mining and getting your ore to R.R. would be so great that the showing on the property as it stands would not guarantee it. Yours truly, W. T. Farrar."

No more waiting. The men in camp sat around the pot-belly stove in the store and discussed the whole affair. Those mining engineers had hardly spent any time at all at the mines. They had just picked up random pieces of rock anywhere. They probably didn't even know what to look for. Why, there were pieces lying around all over up there that would assay at $25 or $30 any time. If that wouldn't pay for the shipping and working, then what would? Those city engineers hadn't asked anyone's advice about where to look, or how the veins of ore ran, and who would know better than the men who worked those mines for years. They hadn't talked to anyone at all. The whole thing had been a hoax, no better than the New England Tunnel and Smelting Company.

Arthur Crowley, Bob Laird, Jim Hamilton, the Crabtrees, all worked their assessments again that fall. Somewhere, sometime, a legitimate company would come to the mines. Some day it had to happen.

Turn of the century did not bring that company. In 1901 Bill Wallace thought he might have an interested customer. In March and April he and Arthur Crowley had assays run on their Cherokee Mine and they ran as high as $31 gold and $2 silver. Certainly that was high enough to make any mining venture profitable. But the interested customer did not agree, and there were no other takers.

By 1902 and 1903 the revived hopes for the valley were dying again. The miners were growing older and it was not as easy to do the $50 assessment work when nobody else seemed interested in their mines. The Crabtrees went back to their ranch outside of Porterville. Bill Wallace spent his summer vacation on the Coast. Arthur Crowley turned his interests back to his job as County Assessor, to his ranches, to his resort in Mineral King.

*Building Mt. Whitney Power Company dam at Lady Franklin Lake, 1904.*

And yet Crowley, like the others, could not quite give up. He let his children roam the hillsides in the summers, relocating what claims they could find and as the years passed he climbed the mountainsides with them. He relocated the "Young America," the "Cherokee," and the "Silverite." Some day, maybe, some time.

One large company did come to the East Fork of the Kaweah River in the late 1890s. For years, Ben M. Maddox, publisher of the *Visalia Times*, and William H. Hammond, one of the owners of the Visalia City Water Company, had been trying to arouse interest in their idea of using the Kaweah River to generate electricity for their town. The people of Visalia were certainly willing. They would have liked more electric power. But the idea seemed too big, too complicated, too expensive. There was no one in that part of the country who knew how to promote such an undertaking.

Bill Hammond did not know how to promote it, but he had a brother who knew how to engineer it. John Hays Hammond had gone to Yale, had learned electrical engineering and had become

*Inside Power House No. 2 at Hammond near Three Rivers. The electricity generated served several San Joaquin communities.*

one of the world's most successful mining engineers. In 1880 he had been appointed to the U.S. Geological Survey of the California gold fields. Then in 1893 he left for the Union of South Africa to explore the gold, tin, coal and diamond deposits there. While in Johannesburg, he became involved in the controversy of the Boer War. He became so involved that he was arrested and sentenced to death. Diplomatic channels had the sentence reduced to 15 years imprisonment, then reduced again to a heavy fine, and John Hammond was released.

John returned to the United States and went to Visalia to visit his brother. Bill wasted no time. He started talking, and John's next project was decided. They and a group of Visalia businessmen, including Carl and Harry Holley and A. G. and Emory Wishon, formed the Mt. Whitney Power Company.

John Hammond knew many people, influential and moneyed. In

1908 he would decline the nomination for the vice-presidency of the United States. He would attend the coronation of George V of England as the representative of President Taft. Now he would use his connections to finance his project. He had no trouble.

In 1897 the company purchased Atwell's Mill and cut a million board feet of Giant Sequoia lumber for a flume running from Oak Grove to the hydroelectric plant they were building above Three Rivers. They named their power station Hammond, and by June of 1899 the Mt. Whitney Power House No. 1 was in operation.

The flow of the water from the East Fork was good, but John Hammond worried about the effects of dry years. The company decided it should build dams at the lakes above Mineral King and at Wolverton Meadows on the Middle Fork above Giant Forest. In 1896 Wilcox and Moffet had located possible sites for reservoirs. In summer of 1899 the lakes above Mineral King were surveyed by Jim Broder.

The ranchers in Three Rivers and the Central Valley below had never been certain about the whole project. They had been promised that their water would only be used temporarily and then returned to them, but they had been skeptical. Now there was talk that the water would be dammed and held back, restricting the flow to their ranches. They objected.

By 1902 the company had timbered all the Sequoias it needed, and Atwell's Mill was sold to Henry Alles, the son-in-law of Isham Mullenix, the original owner. Then the power company turned to its projected dams. In 1904 and 1905 it started work. Dams were built on Wolverton Creek and at Monarch, Crystal, Franklin and Eagle Lakes above Mineral King. Trails were cut up the mountain sides to the dams.

By this time the old-timers of Mineral King were upset. An ugly flume snaked its way down the East Fork, visible all along the road below Oak Grove. The Giant Sequoias at Atwell's Mill were nothing but stumps. And now the sides of their valley were scarred by trails, zig-zagging their dusty way through the manzanita and higher meadows and forests.

But if the Mineral King people were upset, the Central Valley irrigationists were livid. They brought suit against the Mt. Whitney Power Company, claiming the storage of water denied their rights to it. The court ruled in their favor and prevented the building of any more dams. But the company was granted the use of those already constructed, and Bill Clough was hired to open and close the gates each year to regulate the flow of water.

After the scarring of the trails had been softened by new growth and time had eased the shock over their existence, the Mineral King residents began to realize the benefits. The idea of trails was not new to them. In December 1897 a group of them had met in Visalia and framed a petition to Congress asking for $30,000 to build trails and roads in the Sequoia National Park and Sierra Forest Reserve.

Already there were three trails; one over Farewell Gap; another across Timber Gap and Tar Gap to Hockett Meadows; the third to the White Chief Mine. And these new power company trails and the dams created more to do. Now whole families could take a picnic lunch and go on a hike for a day's outing. The lakes were deeper now and more beautiful, the fishing even better, if that was possible. And those who lived in Visalia could hardly complain. The big enterprise was helping them all.

*The wreckage of the Smith House Hotel after the "San Francisco" earthquake of 1906.*

# NINE

------◆------

# EARTHQUAKE

Running a resort was not all fun and friendships. There were problems involved. Mr. Alles almost always seemed to be late with the mail, by a day or even more. The freight wagons did not always arrive with the supplies ordered. In 1903 the Smith House was ransacked before anyone had arrived in the spring, and the canned goods, dishes, tableware, linens all had to be replaced.

There were constant leaks in the water pipe from Spring Creek. Unexpected overnight guests came each year, especially Sierra Club members who came late to camp and found their supplies already out on the trails.

There was the job of disassembling camp each fall: boarding up the windows; bracing the roofs; taking the canvas top off the dance hall; taking inventory of the Smith House, post office, store, and all the cabins; carrying all the valuables down to Atwell's Mill to be stored over the winter because of the perennial threat of avalanche in the valley.

The avalanche precautions were taken every year and each spring on the first trip into Mineral King, there was always more than a little apprehension. Some years, one or two of the private cabins would be found damaged. But Whiskey Smith seemed to have chosen the site for his hotel well. There was never any sign of snowslides there.

In 1906 all the precautions did not help. On April 18 the "San Francisco" earthquake rocked all of California. The disaster that followed in San Francisco was related to the entire world; smaller disasters throughout the state were known only by those who experienced them. In Mineral King the earthquake triggered massive snowslides from every wall of the valley. The avalanches roared down one mountainside and up the opposite one, across the valley, meeting and sliding over each other, creating their own small mountains of snow and ice.

Not until July 4 could Len Cutler, the resort handyman, work his way up to "camp" and report the damage. There was no resort left. Uncle Len's reports were terse and graphic.

Hew cabin—demolished; Shake cabin—complete wreck; Rock Chimney cabin—walls still standing, roof demolished, three feet of snow inside it; Post Office cabin—floor all right, walls all down; Dance Hall—both ends down and west side down with a thirty foot fir tree lying across it; Log Cabin—knocked sky-west of chimney and crooked, five feet of snow in it; Meat Shoppe—in a heap; Barn—one mass of kindling wood, portion of roof across the river; Hotel (Smith House)—telescoped into one solid mass where the bathrooms were, roof turned halfway around and now stands about thirty feet west of main building in a four foot bank of snow...."

So the list went, on through a half dozen more cabins. Those that were not hurt had been broken into. Some had door casings forced off, one door was split, others had the chains cut. Not one escaped damage.

Uncle Len tried to salvage what he could. He cleared away debris so the sun could melt the snow more quickly and whatever was under it could be found. By July 18 there was still three feet of snow in the middle of the ruined hotel. Len dragged parts of stoves and lamps, dishes and beds, into the open. He took inventory of what he found. It was a nasty job.

"Having my feet wet so much it is making me feel a little old," he wrote to Arthur Crowley. "I never saw houses torn, twisted, ground and smashed as they are here. I wish you could see them."

Arthur didn't really want to see them, but he made his way up the road, and when he saw the wreckage, he decided he was not defeated.

*Uncle Len Cutler, 1906.*

One of the small cabins near the Smith House had been shunted into the remaining floor of the Post Office Cabin, and that happenstance made his decision. He waded into the snow with Len Cutler and started cleaning up. When the snow had melted enough, they joined the two remnants of the cabins together, added walls and a roof from other wreckage, and Mineral King had a new store and post office, temporary but functional.

The portion that had been the Post Office Cabin became the store and post office with storage of supplies in its attic. The other cabin, with a partition and door separating it, became living quarters with bunk beds in the attic. There was a definite line across the roof where one side was a little higher than the other, but the two cabins were one and the resort was in business again.

The rest of that summer was spent clearing the wreckage, using some of it to patch what cabins were still standing—the Fisher, Hannah, and Dinley cabins. Other families came up to the valley. Some came to patch or to rebuild their own cabins that lay on government land or on private mill sites. Most looked and shook their heads and abandoned the mess. A few people came in out of curiosity to see what had happened. The pack stations still operated, carrying people in and out on trips into the back country. There was at least a little business.

As if the snowslides had not been misfortune enough, there were quakes from other sources, too. The division of forestry chose that year to file a complaint in a United States court against Arthur Crowley's claim to ownership of the Empire Mill site.

Through the years Arthur had been concerned over the Park and Reserve and their restrictions on mining, hunting, and activities in Mineral King. He had written letters to newspapers and to Congressmen. He had joined with groups protesting the closing of the mountains to open use. In 1895 he had sent a petition to the Department of Interior with the names of all the leading citizens of Visalia on it, asking that he be appointed "Guardian of Sequoia National Park," to protect the citizens' interests. Finally, he had gone into battle with the forestry. Now, in 1906, his actions had brought results.

The forestry's concern was just as real. The early 1900s were a

*"Temporary" store and post office, the center of Mineral King activities after the destruction of Smith House.*

time of abuse. Land was being taken on any pretext, in every manner possible, in large chunks and small. Great land barons were exploiting the government's policy of give-away.

The Homestake Mining Company in the Black Hills of Dakota; Marcus Daly of Anaconda and Butte, Montana; Weyerhauser Lumber of Washington State; all had found methods of amassing thousands of public acres into their private hands. Henry Miller, a California cattleman, could travel through California, Oregon and Nevada and sleep every night on his own land.

As for the railroads, the Southern Pacific alone owned over ten million acres. In 1904 the land entries recorded reached 55,000 acres. The expression, "doing a land office business" had real meaning.

By 1904 the forest service was becoming frightened. If the land entries continued at the going rate, in Oregon alone, within two

[111]

years, there would be no more public timbered lands. The forest supervisors were instructed to check their areas for violators. Anyone claiming lands for purposes other than the entry made, or for obvious future speculation, should be reported.

Harrison White was Supervisor of the Sierra Forest Reserve. He had watched Arthur Crowley building a resort on his Empire Mill site for years. Rather than mining buidings, there was a store, hotel, barn, meat shop, post office and cabins. Rather than miners, whole families from the Central Valley towns went to spend the summer there. In 1904 Mr. White wrote to the General Land Office informing Commissioner Ricnaur of the obvious abuse of the mill site claim.

Arthur Crowley wrote too, requesting a permit to continue occupancy. The commissioner considered the matter. The location notice on the Empire Mill site had been filed before the Forestry Reserves had been formed, before the use of such lands had been restricted. Ricnaur and the Department of Interior granted Special Privilege Case No. 55 for continued occupancy of the buildings on the mill site.

But Supervisor White would not let the matter rest. Arthur Crowley was preparing to apply for patent to the land. White considered this to be an outrageous display of what men could do, and were doing, to take the public lands. In February of 1905 the forest reserves were transferred from the Department of Interior, General Land Office, to the Department of Agriculture. If the Interior had not cared, White decided perhaps the Agriculture would.

On October 2, 1905, Harrison White reported to the Department of Agriculture that forest ranger Harry Wilkinson had made a personal examination of the tract and had found ". . . that there is no mineral on said claim in paying quantities . . .," that the claim had been taken for business purposes, that the mill site was being patented under fraudulent means. A complaint was filed.

On Feburary 21, 1906, the complaint was served and final action on the patent was denied. The first hearing came on July 25. It took until January 15, 1908, for the resulting case of the United States vs. Arthur Crowley to come to court.

Hanna and Miller, the attorneys for the defense, presented an eloquent plea. Based on the fact that the mill site was located before the government reserves placed use restrictions on such claims, the court, on May 14, 1908, awarded Arthur Crowley a favorable decision. On December 17 the patent was granted and signed by Theodore Roosevelt.

Once again the public had lost. The land was taken. The center of one of the most beautiful valleys in the Sierra was now in private hands. Arthur Crowley owned his resort.

*The Mineral King Resort after the earthquake of 1906.*

# TEN

———·—◀◉▶—·———

# AN ARROW IN THE
# HEART OF THE PARK

The automobile came and California had a new frontier. Her people had always been restless, adventurous, moving. That was why they had come west in the first place. Now they could see movements in every direction. The idea of the automobile caught their fancy.

In 1915 a new road started up the East Fork to Mineral King. It began near the Mt. Whitney Power House at Hammond and wound its way up to Oak Grove, on the south side of the canyon, across from the River Hill grade. Near its end at Oak Grove, a beautiful concrete bridge crossed the East Fork to connect the new road to the old one. There was no more River Hill.

"I'll bet there has been more 'cussing' on the old River Hill road than on any road in the world," Arthur said. But it was gone now and autos could reach Mineral King. A new era in the valley's history was about to open. Before it could, history intervened. In April 1917 the United States entered into its first major world war.

The war years affected California less perhaps, than it did other parts of the nation. The state's agriculture was hurt for a time by the Allied blockade of goods, but production rose again as the government demand for food developed. The railroads felt government control for the first time, but never had they been so busy.

[115]

The young men were drafted and left their homes. The purchasing power of the dollar fell. Automobile production turned to planes and guns and ammunition. There was almost no fuel allowed for touring. California's oil fields became important to the nation for the first time. The petroleum industry boomed, but its products all went toward the war effort.

It was a time of great national feeling and patriotism, of restraint in the use of luxuries, of waiting for "the boys" to return. Autos could wait. Time could be taken to grow gardens at home. Meals could do with less meat and sugar and bread. That was about the extent of the war effort in California.

Each summer the same families went up to Mineral King, still in their buckboards or the horse-drawn stage. Talk turned away from mining and more to the war effort, to the hauling away of the Empire machinery to be used for tanks and guns, to the possibilities of peace.

After two years it came. On November 11, 1918, the armistice was declared. It would take four years before formal peace was signed, but the fighting was over. Now a new life could begin. No more restraint. No more waiting. The government regulations eased. In 1919 the food and fuel restrictions were lifted. In 1920 the boys came home, the drafted army released to civilian life.

Mineral King entered the new era. The first automobiles started chugging and boiling and stalling their way up the road, and they made it. They brought more people in, for shorter periods of time. Over the Memorial Day weekend they came in by the dozens.

Arthur Crowley worked at rebuilding his resort. In 1922 he finished a new "hotel" consisting of waiting room, dining room, tent cabins, and bath house. He built and rebuilt several other cabins on his land. He began to advertise throughout the state. Articles appeared in the Visalia, Fresno and Tulare papers. Brochures were sent out describing Mineral King.

The rates were still low: $2.50 per room, per day, per person; $2 each per room, per day, for two persons; breakfast $1; luncheon, $1.25; dinner, $1.50; children under nine, half price; baths 50 cents each; chambermaid service.

No more an all day trip by horse drawn stage. Now, three times a week, the auto stage left the Visalia depot at 8:40 a.m., arriving in Mineral King at 2 p.m., and returning the very same day.

Private cabins started springing up and families came in, sometimes just for the weekend. The road was improved again. On July 22, 1926, the county steam shovel started working on a new road below High Bridge Creek and in 1927 the rerouting of it was completed, eliminating the grade over the highest point on the road. Other changes were made and the road was widened in parts, over Champagne Hill, Swallow Rock Hill, and around Lookout Point, until Arthur Crowley could call it ". . . almost a 'Bully-vard.'"

Crowley tried to keep his resort in tune with the times. In 1921 more water from Spring Creek was piped to more cabins, many of them privately owned by his friends. In 1925 a large sign was set up at Hammond advertising the resort. A soda water cooler was added to the store. In 1925 spring mattresses were put into the tents to replace the old straw ticks. The next year fresh bottled milk was brought in on the stage to sell. Some 60 signs were painted by Arthur for the springs and lakes and trails.

In 1926 a man did some calculating as to the feasibility of bringing an electric "lighting machine" into Mineral King. In 1928 a gasoline operated lighting plant was bought and all the cabins, the dining room, the store, and the waiting room were wired. An electric heater was added to the dining room and a bulb was placed on a big juniper tree outside the store to light the roadway. The sputtering plant was turned on each evening at dusk and off at ten o'clock. In the fall, the electric wires were taken down before the snows came.

The people still gathered in the store after dusk, or at bonfires outside the different cabins. Sometimes the tables were cleared out of the dining room and dances were held. But most often, the evenings were spent in the hotel waiting room. There, talk turned to the new times. Accounts of a car's struggle up the Mineral King road always brought sympathy and laughter. Almost everyone had a radio. In 1926 one was installed in the Mineral King waiting room and the older crowd could spend the evening hours "fishing" for stations, listening to weekly programs, getting annoyed with the static, becoming elated when Maine and Vancouver and Mexico City came in "loud and clear."

There were movies for the younger crowd, for years a nickle a show in the Central Valley towns. In 1926 the first motion picture film in Mineral King was viewed at one of the cabins.

Aviation was a new and exciting adventure. Wild young daredevils went into it, and in July 1927 a group from San Francisco's Crissy Field came into camp. They took over the resort for three days, drinking and gambling. The young girls were excited, their parents worried, and Arthur Crowley wished they hadn't brought their liquor. In 1928 Visalia built an airport and several of the young men in town went up in an "airship" for the first time. Everyone followed the accounts of Lindbergh's flight across the Atlantic.

There were vacuum cleaners and washing machines and electric refrigerators going into the Central Valley homes, all made possible by the advent of installment buying. There was fashion for the women to talk about, silk and rayon hose and the new freedom of less clothing. There were health fads and new religions. There were special celebrations in almost every city of any size. Fresno's Raisin Day and dog and poultry shows always drew big crowds. There were trips to plan and to look back on, tourist magazines to pore through and to dream over. There was the excitement of the new agriculture in California; orange groves and vineyards, walnuts and prunes, and truck farming, made possible by the railways' refrigerated cars.

Events in Mineral King seemed just as exciting. The people who came were always interesting. There were parties all the way from San Francisco, Los Angeles, San Diego, Phoenix. In 1927 Jeff Davis packed a crowd of "real Germans" over Farewell Gap; and that same year 58 members of the Sierra Club made a trip into the valley during which one club member was killed in a fall from a cliff.

There was the Alpine Club with 50 members arriving, and the same summer, an around-the-world hiker arrived in camp. He had started in Rome, had been out 11 years, and planned to take nine more years to finish the trip. There were government officials and mining men, and in the fall there were hunters. Camp was usually

[118]

busy. Sometimes visitors had to sleep in the waiting room. Often every pack animal in the valley was out.

The people who left were just as important as those who came. In 1917 Emma Crowley died and the resort was left to Arthur to manage alone. On April 7, 1925, Uncle Len Cutler committed suicide. Although other handymen came to take his place, none were quite the same. On May 2 of the next year Bill Wallace died at the age of 77.

A fish hatchery was built. In 1927 the Forest Service constructed concrete ponds below the dining room in which they hoped to acclimate planted fish to the high altitude and cold waters. The project was finished on August 13 and water was turned into the ponds. The next day five trucks rumbled into camp from the hatchery at Hammond. Almost the entire camp turned out at dawn to watch 100,000 steelhead fry being poured into the concrete boxes.

The people watched the fish in their new home all that day and all the next, watched them dying. The next year the forestry officials tried again, rebuilding the "rearing" ponds, and this time the experiment succeeded. Until more modern methods of planting came in the 1940s, a favorite afternoon pastime was going down to the fish ponds to watch the fingerlings.

In 1928 there was the fun of an unexpected award. At that time the Mineral King resort was hardly a pretty picture. The cabins, on private and forestry land, had been built for the most part out of salvaged lumber, and they were scattered throughout the valley without plan or restriction. The residents called their structures rustic. The Forest Service decided the whole valley looked like a mess. It ordered the cabin owners to clean up and paint.

Paint they did, until every building in the valley sported a color from pink to purple. The Visalia *Times-Delta* could report that the job was done ". . . with glory to the painters and honor to the resort."

To the amusement of everyone, in November Arthur Crowley received a letter from New York.

"Dear Sir: We have learned through the newspapers that Mineral King has had a campaign with the result that 100% of the houses in town have been painted. We wish to recognize this demonstration of civic progress by presenting the village of Mineral King with an appropriately engraved trophy cup in recognition of this progressive spirit. . . ." The letter was signed R. W. Emerson, Executive Secretary, National Clean-up and Paint-up Campaign Bureau.

The story hit the headlines.

"Mineral King Cleanest Town In State," the Visalia *Times-Delta* bannered. Other newspapers carried the story. *The American City* magazine published an article on it. The silver trophy cup sporting the inscription, "Mineral King, Cleanest Town in California, 1928", was put on display in the window of Gentry's Sporting Goods Store in Visalia. No one ever saw a Forest Service official come to look at it.

Through all the years, the hopes continued. The old miners in Mineral King watched California's output of gold increase to over one million ounces a year, and the price rise to $35.02. They heard of new mining methods and companies that were willing to gamble. Every summer mining men came into Mineral King. Mines were optioned. Fortunes were guaranteed.

In 1912 T. J. Crabtree and W. H. Crabtree gave an option to W. F. Cord of Visalia on their six mines; the Loup claim, White Chief, Lady Franklin, Silver Lake, Silver King, and Dry Bone. Cord was to pay $60,000 for the privilege of working and developing the claims, and was to begin work on or before June 1, 1913.

In 1918 Arthur Crowley and his nephews, Jim and Harry, gave an option to Mrs. O. B. Howard of Sacramento to buy the Empire Discovery, and also the First Extension North and First Extension South owned by Arthur, for a total sum of $100,000 to be paid in full within four years. The mines were to be worked at least $500 worth a year, and the Crowleys were to receive 20 percent on all gross smelter returns.

In 1925 a mining man from San Jose came into camp. Frank Cord was still working on the claims he had bought from the Crabtrees. Samuel Baggs from Glendale became interested in the possibility of investing in the business.

The next year was quiet. Bill Wallace had died and his en-

*Mineral King cabins, 1920*

thusiasm and outside connections were lost. Only Frank Cord came into the valley to work and inspect his mines. But the fall of 1927 brought more excitement. On September 22 two mining men appeared in camp and the next day went up to see the Empire and the Anna Fox. On the evening of October 17 Arthur Crowley entertained a Mr. Herrick at his Visalia home and they talked about the Mineral King mines and a new kind of hydrogen-gas machine used for the extraction of minerals from ores. Perhaps technology could save Mineral King.

The next March Arthur Crowley went down to Glendale in Southern California to talk to Sam Baggs. Six weeks later Baggs decided to lease the Cherokee Mine. In August 1928 Herbert D. Dowell arrived to check the mines, was satisfied with what he saw, and on February 19, 1929, for $340,000 he took an option on nine claims of Frank Cord, Tom Crabtree, and Arthur Crowley. By this time Cord, Crabtree and Crowley owned or claimed almost all of the most promising mines in the district.

In fall of 1929 the Interstate Industrial Transportation Company of Tulare, California, made its bid. C. A. Beinhorn, of Exeter, secured a lease and bond for the company on Cord, Crabtree and Crowley's Anna Fox group. For $100,000, the company bought the Anna Fox, Silver Lake, and Iron Cap. Beinhorn was to receive five percent of all money paid, not less than $5,000, for his services in securing the bond. Cord, Crabtree and Crowley were to receive at least twenty percent of all smelter returns until the $100,000 was paid in full or they would receive that sum within five years. Interstate Industrial was to start work on the mines in the spring, as soon as the snows melted, running a tunnel for 2,000 feet or more until the entire width of the mineral ledge had been cut.

W. T. Perry, Interstate Industrial's secretary, was obviously very serious about the venture. He talked to the three men, wrote letters, and brought mining engineers into camp. But he did not get started on the tunnel. Cord, Crabtree and Crowley decided to give the company more time on its option. In August the tunnel finally started. H. D. Dowell came too, wanting more time on the claims he had leased. A man from the Bureau of Mines came to get information about the different mines to be worked. Forest Service rangers came to check the mineral monuments, the validity of the claims—1930 was a busy year.

In 1931 Jeff Davis and Arthur Crowley found a Mr. Hurlbert who was interested in their Cherokee. Perry and his company continued work and took another engineer to the mines. All the promises in all the options and contracts had brought nothing yet, but that did not discourage anyone. Arthur Crowley wrote in his autobiography that year, "I will have patented land and mining locations in the district from which I expect to make a lot of money." All it would take was time. Mineral King and her miners had waited before. They could wait a while longer.

Always there were threats. The Park wanted Mineral King. In 1891, only one year after it had been formed, the acting superintendent of Sequoia National Park had asked in his report to the Secretary of Interior for the Park's extension.

"The present park is too small to well perform the functions of a game reserve," he wrote, and he proposed that a large portion of the forest lands to the east of the park be taken in. Mineral King was included in the plan.

In 1897 the acting superintendent again urged enlargement. Again Mineral King was included in the plan. The residents of Mineral King began to worry, and Arthur Crowley wrote a letter to the San Francisco *Examiner* concerning parks and reserves and the proposed enlargement.

By 1903 there were proposals to enlarge the forest reserves, too. It was suggested the Sierra Reserve take in the lower foothills including Three Rivers and down to Lemon Cove to protect possible reservoir sites. In 1915 the Kern and Sequoia National Forests were merged again after being split in 1910, but the foothills were not included.

The battles were heated. Some proponents of the Park enlargement insisted that the new portion, incorporating the watersheds of the Kings and Kern Rivers, become a separate park and be named the John Muir National Park. Others insisted one large park could be better administered. All insisted that Mineral King be a part of whatever park was decided on.

The Forest Service formed its own battle lines. There was nothing comprehensive that the administrators of the Sequoia National Forest could plan as long as their boundaries were constantly being changed, and the area of their jurisdiction cut and enlarged and threatened to be cut again. It was not right that Park lands should be taken out of Forest Service areas already under government control.

Moreover, the area contested was hardly park material. It was wilderness, inaccessible, unsuitable for general park development. In 1915 Theodore Roosevelt set aside the first game refuge, and the Forest Service argued that if a game preserve was what people wanted, then such a refuge could be set up inside their jurisdiction. It did not require a park. Fresno needed water from the King's River and Los Angeles wanted water from the Kern. Water management rightfully belonged, not to the Parks system, but to the Forestry. The irrigationists in the Central Valley might lose their water if the Park took over.

The residents of Mineral King formed the third line, and the strength of their opposition to inclusion in the Park surprised everyone. Arthur Crowley took the lead to protect his resort. The old miners and summer families joined with him. "I always was a

*The Mineral King Stage outside the store, early 1900s. The stage ran daily during summer months, bringing visitors and supplies.*

thorn to park officers," Arthur wrote in later years, "fighting all their propositions to include Mineral King in the Park."

In 1911, when the Sierra Club's campaign to enlarge the Park was first started seriously, Arthur Crowley began his own campaign. He and his Mineral King friends wrote letters, talked, argued, published their views. On December 11 the Visalia *Times-Delta* gave their cause a long write-up.

"I am against the enlargement of the Sequoia National Park," Crowley stated. "And every person whom I have spoken to in regard to the matter says: 'No sir, we have all the park we want.' " The Park Service had never treated people fairly once it got its land. It never yet had paid anyone for the patented lands embraced within its boundaries. The proposed enlargement would cut out rangeland and timberland that would be needed by future generations. The park as it stood, had never done anything for fishing. It had left the streams to be stocked by private individuals.

And, most important, ". . . There are numerous bodies of ore within the area of the proposed larger park, and some of it, of not such low grade, either, only waiting for capital to develop it. These bodies of ore will be locked up if put in the park." Arthur Crowley could say with firm certainty that the enlargement ". . . is not desired by even a small minority of our citizens."

The battle went on. The Sierra Club lost its fight for the preservation of the Hetch-Hetchy Valley and concentrated its powers on Sequoia. The National Geographic Society joined them.

In 1915 Mark Daniels, a "government man," came to look the situation over. He told the Mineral King people that they would be able to continue mining if they were included in the park. Only a permit would be required. The government would begin immediate work on a good road through the Park toward Mineral King, and if the park was enlarged, it would spend millions for roads, hotels, and other facilities.

No one believed him. The Park Service had no millions to spend. Daniels was an outsider and it was obvious he couldn't be trusted.

"Don't put all the state into a park, just because a captain, or Daniels or someone else happens to suggest it," Arthur Crowley pleaded. Let the people have some place where they could camp, hunt, fish and enjoy themselves without a permit.

The Park Service tried another line of attack. Arthur Crowley was asked how much he would take to quit fighting. He was asked to sell all his Mineral King property and mineral rights to them. Crowley gave them his price.

"I told Colonel White if they wanted the territory of Mineral King I would take so much. He said it was too much. I said too little or too much, I would take no less."

The price was ridiculous. Arthur Crowley was not going to sell his dreams. But he could spread the story of the "bribe" throughout the state.

The park officials retaliated. They closed the Mineral King road where it passed through their lands, from Lake Canyon to just below Silver City. The Mineral King residents and the Forest Service immediately labeled the action illegal. No one had the legal power to block the right of way of a public road, one that was built long before there was even such a thing as a national park. Adolph Sweet defied the barricade. He passed through it, and others followed. The Park Service did nothing to stop them.

From 1918 until 1926 the Sierra Club increased its efforts until the Sequoia enlargement became its major project. It, the National Geographic Society, along with Stephen T. Mather, worked to acquire private lands within the proposed park area. They sent representatives of their cause to Washington. In 1920 Atwell's Mill was purchased by D. E. Skinner of Seattle, a representative of the National Geographic Society, and it was donated to the Department of Interior.

In 1926 the forces for the status quo both lost and won. On July 3 Arthur Crowley recorded in his diary, ". . . Colonel White visited the camp in the forenoon—learned today that the Sequoia Park was enlarged by about 350 square miles but retained the name Sequoia." The watershed of the Kings Canyon was left out. The valley of Mineral King was not included.

The major reason for enlargement of the park was not only to include more groves of Sequoias, but also to stop destruction caused by the ranging of sheep and the lumbering operations. Mining was not really an issue. Congress decided that if the people of Mineral King wanted their valley, they could have it. But in order to maintain the ecological balance of the area, all hunting must be stopped. Mineral King was made a National Game Refuge.

It was a major victory for conservationists. It was a major victory for summer residents of Mineral King. The hunters, sheepmen, cattlemen, and lumbermen were defeated. The Forest Service had perhaps lost most, but not quite all. And the summers in Mineral King could pass by as they had, no different than they had been before.

The years grew longer. More and more people came and there was never time to rest. Management of the resort began to weigh heavily on the shoulders of Arthur Crowley. When he was 68, after 34 years of running the resort, Arthur decided to retire.

In May 1927 he started looking for buyers. Renick, Wakeham, Dinelly and Phipps, Mrs. Ben Dudley, and a man from Fresno all proved to be prospects. Arthur made his choice. On August 27 he recorded in his diary, ". . . sold my five acres today to Ben Dudley for $15,000." The Dudleys were to take up the option on the property on March 1, 1928.

No sooner had the matter been settled than Tom Phipps and Roland Ross, operators of a pack station in Mineral King, objected. They were afraid the Dudleys would change the character of the camp or that they might sell out to the park. They wanted the valley to remain as it was.

The two men asked Arthur Crowley to wait. If he could give them a little time, they were certain they could get enough people together to raise the money for their own purchase. Crowley wrote to Ben Dudley and told him the matter would have to wait.

Phipps and Ross were slow in gathering their forces, and Arthur was hoping to be relieved of his business that year. On May 28, when it was almost time to reopen the resort for business again, Al and Fred Askin came to him asking about the property. Their interest was a temptation, but Arthur Crowley ran the business again that summer and sold to no one.

In September Al Askin came to Mineral King, looked over the property, stayed overnight with Ben Dudley and talked to him with serious thought of purchase. After the long, busy summer, Arthur was ready to sell. And Ross and Phipps still were not ready to buy. But on October 11 the two packers gathered an interested group together and they came up with $16,000. Finally, on October 30, 1928, Arthur Crowley signed the deed to them for his five acres on the valley floor.

Mineral King was saved. It would not be changed. It would not be spoiled. It would remain the same rustic resort that everyone had grown to know and to love.

There were eleven men in the group of new owners: G. C. Gentry, H. B. McClure, Frank W. Mixter, J. E. Pogue, Frank Pickard, J. A. Moffett, H. A. Hein, J. S. Dungan, C. J. Wilson, Tom Phipps, and Roland Ross. Nine had one-tenth interest, Phipps and Ross had only one-twentieth. But it was basically their resort. They ran it and in 1929 Roland Ross took over the store.

It was not an easy day for Arthur Crowley when, on June 3, he handed over the keys of the store to Ross. On February 1 he had sent in his resignation as Mineral King Postmaster and had asked to have Roland Ross appointed in his place. With a somewhat wistful note he added in his diary that night, ". . . I was appointed in 1897 and held the office continuously ever since."

Still, there were other things to plan. The sale included a 99-year lease on a strip of land in one corner of the five acres where Arthur could build a cabin. As soon as the sale was ready to be finalized, Arthur started drawing his plans for the cabin. On June 22, on his 71st birthday, work on it was begun.

This was no cabin to be put up in three or four days. The first load of lumber for it was so heavy that the truck carrying it broke the bridge coming into camp. It took weeks to get the bridge fully repaired. It took from June 22 to July 12 to get the cabin completed. Even then, the plumbing was not in and the painting was not finished.

But Arthur could not wait for that. For the first summer in 34 years, he could do whatever he pleased. He left Mineral King. He and two of his daughters went to Alaska for a full month's vacation. A new era had dawned.

*Arthur Crowley, 1931, the old man retires*

*Mary Trauger, 1929–"Today am 82"*

# ELEVEN

## ONLY FOR THE FEW

"Ross moved the little old butcher shop," Arthur Crowley lamented in 1930. "One of my old landmarks gone." That was one of the very few changes made in the valley for the next 39 years. They were quiet years. Depression came and all hopes for mining died. There was no money anywhere for development. But still, each summer each mine was relocated and filed on by someone. The tourist business dropped. There was no money for travel. Still each summer the same families returned from the San Joaquin.

In 1932 Arthur Crowley died, and little by little, the other old-timers disappeared; and others took their places to become the old-timers. The seasons came and passed and the troubles of the world passed too, however, Mineral King stayed the same.

In 1939 Ray and Gem Buckman bought Roland Ross' interest in the company, and for almost a quarter of a century, the store, hotel and post office were theirs.

Ray Buckman was no outsider. His father had once been a teamster on the Mineral King road, and his cousin owned one of the pack stations in the valley. Ray had worked for the Broder and Hopping packing concession in Sequoia National Park, and in 1933 he joined with his cousin Phillip as a partner in the Mineral King Packing Company that had been operating since 1901.

Mineral King was as important to the Buckmans as it had been to the Crowleys. They went down to their ranch in Three Rivers each winter, but as soon as the snow had melted on the road they were back in camp. They carried on traditions that had been set. They wanted no big changes either. They were affable and friendly to all who came, caring for the visitor's needs, yet never letting civilization quite take over the valley. It remained rustic, quiet, a world apart.

There were some changes through the years. The misnomer "hotel" was changed to "lodge," and a large sign, seemingly too heavy for the sagging roof, was placed on top of the store. The Buckman packing services were included in the resort's brochures. The prices changed a little. The games of hide-and-seek turned to games of kick-the-can. The dances on Saturday nights moved from the dining room to a big hall down the road at Silver City.

The government set up campgrounds at Cold Springs, Sunny Point, and the Davis Camp near Spring Creek. It gave permits for cabins to be built on Forest Service land and eventually, 100 cabins dotted the valley floor and canyon down through Silver City and into Cabin Cove.

The Civilian Conservation Corps widened trails and repaired dams at the lakes. Hunting returned every few years. The valley game refuge was opened by cooperative agreement between the Forest Service, the Park, and the State Fish and Game Commission to cut the devastation of growing herds of deer. An occasional marked bear came into camp from Sequoia National Park and created excitement and some havoc until a forest ranger could be contacted to kill it.

The beautiful limestone facing of Spring Creek Falls broke and fell into the river in thousands of pieces. The road grew wider each year, the county crews chopping off corners and filling in gullies. Asphalt crept up the dirt grade, a little higher each year, however, the bonfires, the hikes, the evening walks and gatherings at the store, the watermelon feeds, the fishing along the stream, could never change.

The packing business boomed. Ray acted as consultant, trip planner, supplier, and sometimes went out with a party. It was his main interest, his "specialized" business, and there was no better packer than Ray. He kept around 120 head of stock, with packers, guides and cooks. Almost anything anyone wanted on a pack trip the Buckmans would accommodate. The trip could be geared to fishing, hunting, rock climbing, or just sight-seeing. It could last one day or a month, with spot packers taking supplies in and out. It could be large or small, from one person to dozens of people on the Sierra Club trips, to the largest of all when 98 pack animals accompanied the "Trailriders" into the back country.

The people of interest, the experiences, were many. Herbert Hoover's son; Lowell Thomas; James Rolph, the governor of California; the movie actress Jennifer Jones, with her son; a man who flew in from Chile and decided to add a sixteenth mule to his pack train so he could take along a case of Coca Cola. There were times of urgency; taking oxygen to an ailing Sierra Club member at Junction Meadow; packing out eight bodies from a plane crash near Mt. Whitney.

If the Depression of the 1930s brought hard times, the Second World War was a near crisis for Mineral King. Gasoline was rationed and the 60 mile distance from Visalia made the trip a luxury. No more weekend forays up and back. To go meant to stay. Those who lived farther away had to think seriously about going at all, had to scrimp and save their ration cards to make it. Many did, but the tourist business threatened to be lost.

Ray Buckman solved the situation. He applied for a business rationing of gasoline and deployed "guest cars" to several of the Central Valley towns. Those who could reach the San Joaquin could be brought up to Mineral King.

The people started coming again, by bus and by train, from across California, from across the nation; and they came back. Mineral King developed a new kind of inhabitant, the summer tourist "regular." Through the years, the same people would return again and again, from San Diego, from New York, from Chicago. New friendships formed between them and the old summer families. The dates for their arrivals were watched and when a favorite returned, it was an event.

During the 1940s the Department of Agriculture turned its attentions to the valley's fishing. Small log dams were built the length of the upper stream, creating pools for the fish to inhabit.

[133]

Plantings were brought up the road regularly by truck, until in the 1960s, 300,000 trout of catchable size were planted each summer. Air drops were made at the lakes, the planes dropping fingerlings into their waters.

By the 1950s the valley had become an historic site to visit, drawing visitors from places as far away as India. Articles appeared in newspapers and magazines telling of Mineral King's past. A foot worn trail wound its way down to the old fallen stamp mill below Iron Springs. People climbed the sides of Empire Mountain to see the remnants of the tramway and its buckets that lay scattered on the ground; to walk the roadway between the mine and Timber Gap; to explore the caverns of the mine. Those whose parents had been a part of the history became "authorities." They were questioned and they told the stories they had heard, the facts as their families knew them, the fantasies that people had come to believe as reality.

The dreams of mining still continued. During World War II government geologists came into the valley to determine if any of the ores were practical for wartime use. They did find some of possible interest but the idea of mining them never bore fruit. In another year, a private mining interest took over the Lady Franklin mine and stationed armed guards at the entrance of the mine to prevent claim jumping. Their efforts lasted only one summer.

In 1958 the Tulare County Historical Society made an expedition to Mineral King and listened to a talk by Mrs. Robert Christenson. She was a University of California paleontologist whose husband was a geologist in Mineral King doing research for his doctorate. It was her opinion that ". . . the area will never have a big producer in gold, but there is a possibility of commercial deposits of scheelite, a tungsten ore."

The third generation scrambled up the mountainsides in search of the old rock monuments with their rusty tobacco tins. They put relocation notices inside them in their families' names. But the claims were seldom filed now. The children were merely acting out the history of the past.

As the ghosts of the past returned in story and in research, so Mineral King began to look more and more like a ghost town. The paint of 1928 had peeled and faded. Some cabins were repainted.

[134]

Some were not. Roofs began to sag. The porch on the old store drooped. No more avalanches came to destroy, but the weight of time took its toll.

The tourists of the 1950s and '60s were changing with the times. They began to expect more out of the accommodations where they would spend their one vacation a year. They had more to spend on that vacation. In Mineral King the sputtering lights still went out at 10 o'clock. The water that came from the faucets often had air and sediment in it. The flooring creaked. The heating was inadequate. The trails to the lakes and mineral springs were deteriorating.

In 1950 the condition of the resort was such that even the times of rising inflation could not raise prices. The rates were almost as low as, and in some cases, lower than they had been in the 1920s: tent cabins, bedding furnished, one person per day, $1.50; two persons per day, $2; housekeeping cabins, fully equipped except bedding, two persons per week, $15; breakfast, $1; luncheon, $1.50; dinner, $2. Mineral King began to be called "primitive" by some people. At least the accommodations were primitive. Even the plumbing was historic.

The responsibilities of the decaying old resort were beginning to weigh as heavily on Ray Buckman's shoulders as they had on Arthur Crowley's. In 1957 Ray sold the Mineral King Pack Station to Lee Maloy. For years Ray's daughter and son-in-law, Barbara and Jack Hansen, took over the running of the store and lodge. Then their own growing responsibilities forced them away. In 1961 Ray and Gem leased the store to Bill and Marilyn De Carteret. For 22 years Mineral King had been the Buckman's—now they too could rest.

The people who built cabins and spent their summers in the valley were not the only ones interested in maintaining the status quo. The conservationists who came through the valley on their way to the back country began to know Mineral King. To have a beautiful area so close to civilization and yet so lacking in civilization was a charm.

The Sierra Club had been formed by John Muir and several of his friends from the San Francisco area in 1892. The club's purpose in the beginning was simple: "To explore, enjoy, and render accessible the mountain regions of the Pacific coast; to publish authentic information concerning them, to enlist the support and cooperation of the people and the government in preserving the forests and other natural features of the Sierra Nevada."

As early as 1903 the club publicized its interest in Mineral King. William H. Dudley wrote in the *Sierra Club Bulletin*, ". . . There is nothing in the whole Sierra range more beautiful than the valley of Mineral King in June; nothing more like an upper valley in the Swiss Alps."

Attesting to the valley's importance as a jumping off point into the back wilderness country, he included a view of Farewell Gap and predicted, ". . . Through it will pass the long cavalcades of the Sierra Club, as many have done before; it is the great thoroughfare of the Southern Sierras."

Through the valley the long cavalcades of the Sierra Club did come. Year after year it was planned as one of the starting points for their high Sierra trips. The more the club's members came, the more they knew the valley, the more they cared about it and its future.

The enlarging of Sequoia National Park in 1926 was due in no small part to the efforts of the Sierra Club. When Mineral King was not included, there was disappointment. Thereafter, several of the club members took a keen interest in the development of the valley. It was not by chance that the phrase, ". . . to render accessible . . ." was deleted from the club's list of purposes when the automobile threatened to make the forest lands too much so. With Mineral King there was no exception. The actual lack of development, the deterioration of the resort, was better than having the valley overrun.

Sierra Club members, like some tourists, started calling Mineral King primitive, a "de facto" wilderness. They did not mean the facilities, however, they meant the delicate beauty of the valley; the meadowlands and quiet forests; the falling streams that could only exist as they had through the ages if civilization was kept out.

# TWELVE

———◆———

# WHITE GOLD

After 90 years of hopes and dreams, it was all officially ended. In 1963, based on the opinion of the United States Attorney General relating to the mineral locations in the Wichita National Forest Game Refuge, the officials of the Sequoia National Forest determined that mining was no longer legal in Mineral King. The decision was made in response to an inquiry from Herbert D. Dowell of Beverly Hills, California, one of the men who had taken options on the mines in the 1930s.

"It is our position," the forestry officals stated, "that the Mineral King area in Sequoia National Game Refuge is not open to prospecting and mining location." Such a decision was not surprising. For more than a decade, government lands had increasingly been closed to mining use. There were good reasons. In 1955 new mining claims were being filed on the national forests at the rate of seven an hour, or 5,000 every month. In one month 100,000 acres were staked out to mining claims. Most were being used for every purpose but mining: gas stations, homesteads, summer camps, future speculation.

On July 23, 1955, Public Law 167 was passed in Congress. It closed mining to sand, stone, gravel, pumice or cinder. It allowed the government to timber and graze on mining claims. And it gave the forestry a greater measure of control over all claims. The Forest

[137]

Service responded by closing several areas and by watching accepted claims more closely. In 1963 it closed the Mineral King District.

Perhaps this was the end. Mining interest in Mineral King had died years ago anyway, with the Depression, with the passing of its original believers, and with the failure of more recent attempts. Now it could never be revived. Perhaps the valley was destined to continue its sleepy existence forever.

Almost no one believed that. There may have been reasons why Mineral King should be closed to mining, but for twenty years, another dream had been building. If there was not gold and silver to be made into bullion, there was "white gold" that could be made into money—there was snow.

Realization of such a dream inevitably took time. It had begun when the first ski was put on the foot of man as far back as the stone age. What was winter necessity for travel in the northlands became progressively a means of hunting, of waging battles, of competition. The joy of flying down a hill, of sliding cross country on a sunlit day, of climbing a snow covered mountain that could not otherwise be climbed, of racing for the thrill of speed or to prove stamina, endurance, and bravery, all this made skiing more than a necessity. It became a way of life. It became a sport.

For centuries, Europeans had skied and improved their skis and even held competitions. But it was not until the 1880s, just when hopes were dimming for a mining bonanza in Mineral King, that skiing became a modern sport. Sondre Norheim of Norway invented the modern ski binding, and in 1881 the world's first ski school was opened in Oslo, Norway.

Even before then people of California and Mineral King knew of skiing. Skis were first used in Wisconsin in 1841, but it was John A. "Snowshoe" Thompson who brought them to California. Since 1856 Snowshoe had carried mail across the Sierra Nevada from Genoa, Nevada, to the west slope communities, and in winter he had accomplished the task on skis.

Snowshoe Thompson had also interested some of his friends in skiing as a sport. On Sundays, in clear weather just for the fun of it, they would race down the snowy hills on their twelve foot boards, guiding themselves with long poles held between their legs.

[138]

W. O. Clough en route to the Empire cabin with his "skees", in
October of 1916.

In Mineral King during winter of 1878 Harry Trauger and the other employees of the New England Company used "skees" to get from the mines down to the valley floor. Throughout the years, Bill Clough used them for winter travel in the valley. In 1905 the *Sierra Club Bulletin* published an article explaining the exact method for making such "skees."

In 1924 skiing was made an Olympic sport and in 1932 the Winter Olympics were held in the United States, at Lake Placid, New York. By 1935 California had its Badger Pass, Blue Ridge and Soda Springs ski areas, and it was estimated that in California alone, the ski industry had become a ten million dollar business.

Still, it was not until after the World War II that skiing got a real start in the United States. Suddenly, overnight it seemed, it became a major industry. And no sooner had that happened than eyes turned to Mineral King.

Since 1873 snow had been nothing but a problem and a curse in Mineral King. There were always avalanches and snowslides, the washing out of the road, delays in the spring opening, the yearly anxiety over whether mining facilities or cabins or the resort might have been crushed or damaged over the winter. The valley gathered too much snow.

But for skiers there is rarely such a thing as too much snow. As the young people of Tulare County began to strap on skiis and learn the sport, they began to talk about Mineral King. For the first time since 1881 the valley experienced winter visitors. Young men would drive as far up the road as possible, and when snow blocked their path, they would ski the rest of the way into the valley. Then they they would climb again, up the mountainsides, all for a run or two in the untouched powder.

It was unbelievable. Never had they seen so much snow. What had seemed a closed and narrow valley in summer opened into wide snowfields and ski runs in winter. And if Mineral King was beautiful in summer, it was breathtaking in winter. It was a skier's paradise.

The word was not kept a secret. As far back as 1933, the year after the Winter Olympics were staged at Lake Placid, talk had started of Mineral King being the greatest potential ski area in the United States. In winter of 1937 Otto Steiner, one of the greatest cross country skiers of the world, discovered Mineral King. For years he spread the news, and others came after him. In 1946 Hannes Schneider and Luggi Foeger conducted a ski survey of California and Nevada and they reported that Mineral King offered the best skiing in the entire area.

In October of 1946 Alf Engen, Scandinavian skier and coach of the United States Olympic ski team, made a trip into Mineral King. His report held no reservations. There was no alpine area comparable, he told the world. Skiing often could begin as early as October and continue through June. The high peaks would give wind protection to the valley. The potential ski slopes were the best in the world.

If there were problems involved, they could be overcome. There were only two potential slide areas and they could be contained with the construction of snowsheds. The avalanche danger at Sun Valley, Idaho, was much more serious than it would be in Mineral King. And the road? Certainly it would be difficult. But the road into Giant Forest had posed a greater problem than one into Mineral King would. There was no doubt that some day Mineral King would become a ski resort.

The residents of Tulare County could see what their fathers and grandfathers had seen in 1874. If a boom came to Mineral King, it would come to them, too. It was time to take action.

The skiers looked to their own special organization. In 1946 the California Ski Association formed a special Mineral King Committee under the leadership of Mr. Fay Lawrence of Los Angeles. The committee's aim was to bring national and governmental attention to the Mineral King Valley. More ski experts were invited to take a look. Fred Iselin, Sun Valley ski instructor, and Otto Lang came, and they both enthusiastically declared that nowhere in the United States were snow conditions better. Mineral King was equal to or better than any place in the Alps.

In 1947 the Tulare County Board of Supervisors, the Forest Service, the Ski Association's Mineral King Committee, and the Sierra Club pooled their interests and resources. The county appropriated $5,000 for a study of the valley's ski potentials and the other organizations donated money, time, experience, and their publicly declared backing. Plans for a detailed winter survey of the valley were begun. The state and federal governments were asked to consider proposals for an all-weather highway into Mineral King. Citizens of the county were approached with the idea of a toll road to be financed by bonds. The feasibility of a cog railroad from Hammond was discussed.

In October 1947 Ludvig (Vicki) Hasher, his wife Bea, and young Kurt Barthel arrived to conduct the winter survey. Vicki Hasher was experienced. Not only was he a well known skier, but in the winter of 1925-1926 he had conducted a similar winter survey in the Silvretta Range of the Austrian Alps. On November 1 the party of three began their work.

For the first time since 1878 the valley was inhabited all winter long. In that winter the Traugers, along with several other workers of the New England Company had stayed, and as the years passed the Traugers had continued to go into Mineral King in the winter. On snowshoes or on "skees," they would go up the mountain to check the Empire Mine and to work it, until the snows became too deep. Mary conducted her own snow surveys. One winter she marked the snow level on a juniper tree south of the store that was eventually built, and the next summer the mark showed that the snow had been fifty feet deep.

The avalanche of 1878 had destroyed the New England Company's boarding house where the Traugers and the other men were staying that winter. Now in 1947 the Hashers and Barthel moved into the Mineral King Guard Station headquarters. Its placement was almost the exact location where the boarding house had stood.

But this time winter was no threat. California experienced the most severe drought it had had in more than 70 years. December passed with no snow. January came and still the big storms did not materialize. Finally in February the pattern broke. By the end of the season, snowfall in the Sierra nearly reached the normal mark, but it had not been a heavy winter.

In spite of the bad year, reports of the survey were all good. When storms did come, Mineral King received more than her share of snow. Maximum snowpack reached 74 inches in the valley and 108 inches in the higher bowls. When there was snow, it was excellent. Because of the mild winter, temperatures had been warmer than usual and avalanches were not a danger. But in any year, the high peaks and ridges protected the valley from wind so the snow could fall heavily. Even in the higher bowls winds were not as strong as had been expected.

The Hashers and Barthel stayed for six months, checking snowfall, temperatures, wind velocities, stream flow, snow conditions, avalanches, skiing conditions, and the suitability of possible ski runs. They came to one major decision: "Mineral King has superlative ski terrain."

There were ten possible runs with good snow conditions and they ran up to three and a half miles long with up to 4,000 feet vertical descents. Hasher laid out a possible Olympic ski run from Sawtooth Peak down to the valley floor and found generally good conditions in the White Chief Bowl and Farewell Gap areas.

"Take six Sun Valleys," he said, "and lay them end to end and you have the skiable areas of Mineral King."

The report concluded that avalanches could be controlled, even in heavy winters. There was sufficient water to sustain a resort. The terrain and snow conditions were excellent. Large amounts of money would be needed for development. An all-weather road should meet the standard stipulated for trans-Sierra State highways.

Such a report was bound to bring action. But somehow nothing happened. In November of 1948 the Visalia *Times-Delta* ran an editorial. Sun Valley had been developed. Why not Mineral King?

"Other states and communities in the west are not letting this gold mine of winter sports money get away from them. Mineral King! The name practically sells itself. Tulare County: from snow to cotton in 40 miles. Let's develop Mineral King and tell the world."

As always since the valley's first discovery, there was that same problem to hurdle—that of transportation.

In the next winter of 1948–1949 the Hashers returned to the valley and continued their study. Ray Buckman opened the resort to winter use for the first time. People came in on skiis and sno-cats and a big DC 6 tractor that pulled a sled behind it.

The valley floor was checked for possible airplane landing sites. *Collier's Magazine* sent writers in to do an article. A party of thirty people including ski enthusiasts, radio and newspaper men, cham-

*Winter 1949, on top of the Big Rock, Timber Gap in background.*

bers of commerce representatives from the Central Valley towns, San Francisco, and Los Angeles, was brought into the valley in January by Ray Buckman. Fay Lawrence of the Mineral King Committee talked to several parties who seemed interested in developing the area. Cortland Hill, a railroad magnate, was one of them.

In September 1949 the Forest Service announced it would accept applications until February 1950 from individuals or firms who could show ability to operate a resort and ski facilities at Mineral King. Any successful applicant would be granted a special use permit in return for payment of an annual fee.

The prospectus included plans for a hotel to accommodate 150 persons; a chair lift, one mile long; a "T-Bar" lift, 2,100 feet long; other facilities with cost to exceed $300,000; "over-the-snow" transportation between highway 198 and the resort wherever snow removal on the old road was not feasible; all construction in the resort to be completed within two years.

After all the excitement and gossip about who might be interested, there were no takers. One bid was received, but after further consideration of the access problems, even it was dropped. "Over-the-snow" transportation into the valley would be too expensive and too limited. And it was estimated that to build a new all-weather highway would cost between two to four million dollars or even more. If access to the valley had been solved in 1874 and 1879, it seemed impossible now in 1949.

The years passed. Interested people still came to inspect the valley. They talked of its potential. They stirred new rumors. Congressman Harlan Hagen of Tulare, Kings, and Kern counties, held hearings on possible development. In 1953 Hugh Wolfe Frank of Germany proposed a five year project to build a road into the valley and start a development. The name of Walt Disney was increasingly heard among the rumors.

Walt Disney had long been interested in skiing. He had learned the sport in the 1930s at Badger Pass, had bought the first stock issued in the Sugar Bowl Ski Corporation near Donner Summit, and had one peak there named for him. In 1960 he staged the opening of the Winter Olympics at Squaw Valley, California. Seeing the skiing interest generated there, he asked Olympic champion skier and Denver University ski coach, Willy Schaeffler, to go take a look at Mineral King. Schaeffler looked and decided ". . . Mineral King has the largest, finest skiing areas grouped in a compact region that I have ever seen. Nothing in America, Europe, or anywhere else in the world compares with it." Walt Disney went to look too, and he agreed. Still nothing happened. The road was too large a stumbling block.

Two years later, the rumors mushroomed again. In 1962 a combine of Southern California promoters and resort developers began studying plans to build a monorail into the valley which would be capable of carrying up to 20,000 skiers a weekend. A Los Angeles company bought land near Hammond, close to the Mineral King road, a location obviously suitable for a monorail terminal. Forest Service officials admitted they had heard of such plans. But they had heard many plans before.

There was no action in 1964, only persistent rumors, but the valley still had its believers. "It is certain," Gem Buckman wrote, "that this beautiful mountain area has a future even more vital and exciting than its past."

Once again, Mineral King and its believers could wait.

It came by request. Robert Brandt and his wife, actress Janet Leigh, asked the Forest Service to reopen Mineral King for bids. Their group submitted a feasibility study of the area's ski potentials in January 1965. They had sent snow experts Monty Atwater and Ed La Chapelle into the valley to conduct avalanche surveys. Satisfied with the findings, they decided they could raise enough money to build a resort and exert enough influence to get a road.

For once all rumors seemed to be coming true. All the "big ski" people, all the "big money" people who had visited the valley in the past few years came again to attention. Not only had Brandt been sending experts in to investigate, representatives of Walt Disney had been bargaining since 1963 to buy all the private land in the valley.

The Forest Service took up the challenge and in February 1965, it issued another prospectus. The costs outlined were not just to exceed $300,000 as they had in 1949, this time the money bid for the resort would have to be enough to justify the building of a road.

The 1965 prospectus called for a development of three million dollars minimum; lifts or tramways with a capacity of 2,000 persons per hour; parking for 1200 automobiles; a resort, to be built on private land, with overnight accommodations for at least 100 individuals; and the Forest Service to receive a minimum of two percent of all receipts for a thirty year term permit including a three year probational lease. The prospectus outlined eight major ski basins, suggesting that White Chief, Eagle, and either Farewell or Mosquito bowls be developed in the first phase.

It would take monumental planning and monumental funding. The road was still a problem and the Forest Service could not take responsibility for that. The successful bidder would have to get a firm commitment on an all-weather highway before the three year provisional lease expired.

The prospectus warned, "Cost of relocating and improving the road to a winter access standard is estimated to exceed five million dollars. No public agency is obligated to undertake the road project, and the successful proponent will have to make appropriate arrangements." Residents of Mineral King saw another dream about to crumble. The proposal sounded impossible.

Many of the people were thankful. It was inconceivable to imagine their valley being overrun with tourists both summer and winter. Others were disappointed. The resort was looking more and more like a shanty town, and it seemed Mineral King's potential would never be realized. If a smaller proposal had been made, at least something might have been started. Still, there was some reason to believe it could happen. Ray Buckman was contacted about sale of his resort property, was confidentially advised of the certainty of development and he commented calmly that it could be ". . . the biggest thing that ever hit Tulare County."

Bids were opened on August 31, 1965, and even Ray Buckman had to be astounded. Not only was there a bid from Robert Brandt, there was also one from Walt Disney, whose agent, Robert B. Hicks, had successfully and quietly bought almost all the private land in the valley between 1963 and 1964.

There were six bids in total: Brandt's Mineral King Development Company with Lowell Thomas and Union Oil Company president Fred L. Hartley on the board of directors; Disney's WEB Corporation, with Olympic director of ski events, Willy Schaeffler; Mineral King Recreational Corporation of Beverly Hills, headed by Raul Balderas as company secretary and Chris Kuraisa, the developer of Heavenly Valley; Don Bollenbacher and Associates of Los Angeles; Marcon Construction and Associates of La Crescenta, headed by Dave Ward; Ragnar C. Qvale and Associates, Architects, of Los Angeles, with brother sportsman, Kjell H. Qvale of San Francisco.

Not only were the number of bids surprising, the scope of the developments planned was overwhelming. Forest Service official, W. S. (Slim) Davis announced, "In the history of the forest service we have never had a response like this. It is the largest thing of its kind."

Three million dollars? Disney came up with 15 million for the first phase with 35 million or more by the mid-1970s. Brandt's plans called for an initial 15 million with full development estimated at 40 million. Balderas and Kuraisa called for 7 to 8 million with up to 42 million tentatively raised for full development.

Bollenbacher planned 3 to 8 million initially with final development "geared to demand." Marcon Construction gave no estimates, but sent plans for full development of all eight ski bowls. Qvale figured development costs "in the millions" with no way to present figures until plans were completed with Forest Service advice and cooperation. For the first time in its history, Mineral King hit the national headlines. The greatest ski area in the United States, or perhaps in the entire world, was about to be born.

Sequoia Forest Supervisor Lawrence Whitfield was assigned to review the bids and send his recommendations to San Francisco. There, Regional Forestry Director Charles Connaughton was expected to make a final decision within 30 days.

But the whole concept had become too large. As one official said, "Mineral King grew up too fast." Whitfield and Connaughton sent the bids to Washington D.C.

A long period of waiting began. On October 1, 1965, the original deadline for the decision passed. On October 20 the San Francisco *Chronicle* reported, "Mineral King Ski Area Winner Due 'Any Day.'" But Secretary of Agriculture Orville L. Freeman found the decision as difficult as had Whitfield and Connaughton. On October 26 it was said that three of the bids met with the minimum government criteria. The decision in favor of one of them would be forthcoming soon.

On October 27 Freeman finally announced that he had eliminated four bids and had chosen Brandt and Disney proposals as the "finalists." He appointed a three man committee to review the two offers, meet with representatives of the two companies, then make a final recommendation. The panel included Assistant Secretary of Agriculture, John Baker; Executive Assistant, Thomas Hughes; and Chief of the U.S. Forest Service, Edward Cliff.

More waiting. Both proposals projected more than twice the minimum requirements stated in the prospectus. They were large proposals and they were complex. The government needed to know exactly how the plans were to be carried out, exactly what the financing was, what the capacity of the facilities would be.

In the meantime, both Brandt and Disney began a public campaign. Disney contacted and pressured Governor Brown of California concerning the road. He sent Robert Hicks throughout California in an attempt to publicize the Disney plan.

It was estimated by Disney that the resort would add $570 to $600 million to the state's economy within the next 10 years. And that figure would soar to one billion dollars in 15 years. Twenty-five million would be spent annually in Mineral King by tourists, and another 25 million in the San Joaquin Valley. Two and one-half million people would visit the valley annually, 400,000 in the winter, and 2.1 million in the summer. By 1978 the resort would add $100 million in payrolls to the surrounding area, paying taxes of $2.1 million to California and $1.5 million to Tulare County.

The most important aspect of Disney's proposal, however, was his interest in conservation. He pledged to preserve the great natural beauty of the site while establishing a year-round recreation facility for everyone, ". . . regardless of age, income, leisure-time interest or athletic abilities . . . suited to every pocketbook."

Although there would be 14 ski lifts in the final development, only one would be seen from the valley floor. Service facilities would be placed under the village. No automobiles would be allowed on the actual valley floor. As few trees would be cut as feasibly possible. The resort area would blend in with the natural

[149]

surroundings and would be placed at the entrance on the north end of the valley, preserving most of the valley's natural beauty.

Walt Disney's plan became the sentimental favorite. But the government seemed to have no favorite, and it was in no hurry. On November 12, the Visalia *Times-Delta* reported to the anxious public, "Mineral King Contract Decision May Be Weeks or Even Months Away."

On December 7, the Three Rivers Chamber of Commerce asked Governor Pat Brown's aid in convincing the Department of Agriculture to end the delays. Finally, on December 17, 1965, after over two months of waiting, the announcement was made. Mineral King was Walt Disney's.

The full plans were unfolded to the public. For duration of the three year interim lease, there would be a research and development phase, and all preliminary work would be completed. Snow and weather surveys were begun, as well as studies on soil, water, and resort plans. A snow study team for the first winter was composed of Willy Stark and Gary Poulsen and their wives. The next winter, Dave and Susan Beck and John and Alice Blair were sent in. Avalanche sheds were to be built, trails reworked and improved. The road was to be started, perhaps small ski lifts installed and helicopter and sno-cat service maintained during the interim.

By October 1973 the resort would be a reality. Final plans called for 14 ski lifts encompassing 1500 acres of land. They would provide ski slopes classified from beginner to expert, giving access to the alpine heights for summer visitors. A three tiered parking facility near the entrance to the valley would accommodate 2500 vehicles. A high capacity public conveyance would carry people to the resort.

The village would be completely self-contained. It would have a chapel, an ice skating rink, swimming pools, convenience shops, a theater, conference center, post office, general store, cafeterias and restaurants, and two major hotels, one luxury and one medium priced.

There would also be living quarters for employees, a hospital and first aid station, an automobile service center, a fire station and heliport. All would be done in an "American Alpine" architecture blending in with the area. Ski lifts woud be camouflaged and

[150]

situated so as not to be seen from the valley entrance. Service areas, as had been promised, were to be placed underground. By the winter of 1978 – 1979, the master plan would be completed with a total expenditure of $35 million. But there was still that perennial problem of the road. Even as the Disney corporation began the preliminary work for the resort, the road remained a question.

On July 31, 1965, while bids were still being received, the Mineral King road, a substandard county road, was placed in the California state highway system. The next spring in April 1966, after the contract had been awarded to Disney, a state aerial survey for the routing of an all-weather highway was conducted. Cost of the reconstructed highway was figured at $15 million. In August the California Division of Highways finished its preliminary studies and it was announced the proposed road would cost $20 million.

Earlier that year an engineering firm surveyed a route for a possible tunnel to carry electric trains from Dillonwood, near Balch Park, through Farewell Gap and into Mineral King. The cost for such a project was estimated at $19 million, plus improvement of a road to Balch Park. Such a railroad would not disturb the mountain wilderness; it would not be affected by winter storms, but it would be just as expensive as a highway and it could possibly open up the back country of the Little Kern to future roads and development.

On September 17 the road costs soared even higher. Governor Edmund G. (Pat) Brown announced that the State of California and the federal government would build a $25 million highway into Mineral King. In October the federal Economic Development Administration approved a $3 million grant for the road. Brown filed an application for another $9 million, and asked the California State Legislature to approve funding for the balance of the $25 million, $1 million per mile.

Then disaster struck. The resort plans had been approved and funded; the highway plans had been approved and potentially funded; and the man who had made such miracles come true was lost. On December 15, 1966, Walt Disney died.

Questions were raised, doubts expressed. With Walt gone, would the plans die, would they be changed, would the Department of Agriculture honor them?

The questions were answered, the doubts quieted. Walt's

[151]

brother, Roy, took over as head of operations. Nothing would be changed. A well trained organization had been set up to develop Mineral King, and it would continue. Walt Disney had left the world a large inheritance of wonders and hopes and dreams, and those dreams would not be left to die.

The next year the State Highway Commission, confident of the Disney Productions' sincerity, committed $20 million in highway funds for a two lane, all weather highway with passing lanes to be built to Mineral King. The vote of the commission was five to two, with three men arguing it should be made a toll road. Completion was called for by October 1973.

In May 1968 the United States Department of Interior, under Secretary Udall, gave its preliminary approval for construction of the road through the 9.3 miles of park lands. Work was started acquiring the necessary right of way for it and for electric transmission lines to cross the park to the resort.

Approval for the project was given with the understanding that the final authorization would be granted only after the California Department of Transportation, working with the Park and Forest Services, had developed means of constructing the roadway without in any way jeopardizing National Park value, including the Giant Sequoia trees, and without creating any major erosion, sedimentation, or pollution.

At last the great problem that had plagued the valley for nearly a century appeared to be nearing a solution. Mineral King's potential was on the brink of becoming a reality.

Walt Disney was not the only conservationist whose influence was to affect the valley. The Sierra Club still maintained its interest. If Disney believed conservation meant opening the valley to its fullest use while preserving its natural beauty, the Sierra Club believed no such thing was possible. No sooner had the awarding of the lease been decided than the Sierra Club began a full scale fight against it.

For years the club had called for development of the valley. It had lent its support to the 1947–1948 winter survey. In its battle against the opening of the San Gorgonio ski area in the wilderness area of the southern California mountains, it had suggested de-

[152]

velopment of Mineral King instead. But now that the scope of the Mineral King project became apparent, the club reversed its policies.

No longer was Mineral King the perfect place for skiing. Now it was a fragile and narrow valley which could be destroyed by the impact of more than two million visitors a year. No longer was Walt Disney the great conservationist who had been given an honorary membership in the Sierra Club in 1955 for his ". . . magnificent contributions to a widespread appreciation of our wildlife."

Now Disney threatened destruction of that very wildlife in a national game refuge. He was creating another "Disneyland" in a "de facto wilderness." He was bringing millions of people to the edge of the real wilderness, the high Sierra back country, and giving them the opportunity to pour into that country.

Many of the residents of the area agreed. Those who had cabins at Faculty Flat, those who had leased land from the Forest Service for their summer homes, were going to lose them. Those whose families had been able to go into Mineral King each year to enjoy its unchanging quality of peace and isolation were going to see their valley overrun. Those who had packed out of the valley into the back country to meet with nature and escape civilization would find that very civilization crowding the trails beside them.

The Mineral King District Association was formed. It was composed of cabin owners and interested people in the area, and it began enlisting local sympathy and aid for its cause. It opposed the entire project, calling for public hearings, claiming no adequate study of the valley had preceded issuance of the prospectus, that nothing could stop a "Disneyland" type of development, that the road was too costly, that there undoubtedly would be water pollution.

Other organizations joined the cause: the National Parks Association, the Wilderness Society, even the Santa Maria Riding and Roping Club. The Sierra Club led the fight. Early in September 1965, even before the development bids had been opened, it first publicly opposed the project. The club directors met and issued a statement. They felt development would harm the fragile, high alpine area, that the area was logically a part of Sequoia National

Park and was too important to be spoiled with massive development. These statements were to be the basic theme of protest for the next five years.

The club's opposition to development was more in line with their philosophy than had been the earlier approval of a ski complex. "Wilderness conservationists believe that the uses of nature go beyond consumption," Philip Hyde wrote in the November 1958 issue of the *Sierra Club Bulletin*. "In seeking to interpret and explain the uses of nature, we must emphasize qualitative experience . . . we do not need to worry about the wild lands going to waste if commercial values to be gained from them are not harvested. It is not the land that suffers from not being used, it is the people. Wilderness conservation means, primarily, conservation of the spiritual values of the wild lands, for human beings."

What human beings, the proponents of the Mineral King development asked, and for how many? How many would be allowed in to enjoy the valley and how many would be barred from it?

It was obvious that it would be difficult to bar those who wanted to come. The September 17, 1965, issue of the Hanford *Sentinel* carried an editorial about the problem. Since the first publicity concerning development of the valley, people had been pouring in.

"And even though the road into Mineral King is so terrible that only the most determined are willing to make the effort," the editorial lamented, "the tiny valley is all but overrun with summer visitors."

The problem grew worse each year. Cars streamed up the twisting, rutted road that narrowed to one lane in many places, most of it basically the same road that had been carved out of the canyonside for wagons in 1879. The campgrounds in the valley filled and overflowed and camping vehicles settled in the open meadows.

The Forest Service was loathe to develop more campgrounds until full plans for the valley's development had been completed. It tried to regulate and contain the people, but the problem grew larger and more difficult until in 1970 an announcement was made that restrictions were being issued on camping and vehicle usage. Camping was to be restricted to two specified sites and the road would be closed at the pack station. Until development, only a fortunate few would be able to go to Mineral King.

[154]

*Sawtooth Peak, winter 1949*

In the November 1967 issue of the *Sierra Club Bulletin*, the club outlined its reasons for opposition to the development. Disney Productions, the Forest Service, the Far West Ski Association, Chambers of Commerce, newspapers, and private citizens answered the allegations.

The Sierra Club stated, "The project is poorly conceived, Disney's Mineral King plan is too big. Population pressures would destroy the fragile character of the valley."

The opposition argued that population pressures were already destroying the fragile valley. As more publicity was published over the controversy, more and more people would go to see Mineral King for themselves. With the population of California growing, even more visitors would come. Without planned facilities and a planned future, the valley could be destroyed.

"As matters stand now," Mineral King pack station operator, Bill De Carteret said, "more and more people are making a mess of the country. By setting up a good program, people can enjoy everything."

The second issue involved transportation. "The development would bring too many cars into Mineral King Valley. A 25 mile, dead-end, access road would be choked. Groves of Sequoias would be affected."

"Disney's plan states unequivocably that no cars are to be allowed in the valley," came the answer. Adequate parking facilities at the valley entrance would handle all vehicles with ease. No redwoods would be destroyed for the new road. The major portion of the valley floor would remain untouched.

"The project is not planned with the protection of Sequoia National Park in mind," the article next stated. Opposing interests, however, claimed that the project was being planned with the full cooperation and aid of the Park Service. It was planned partly as a protection to Sequoia National Park.

"There needs to be development on the fringes of the great national parks to accommodate the people," the Hanford *Sentinel* editorialized. "Otherwise, it can be seen, the unrelieved pressures for use will overrun the great natural preserves and perhaps eventually force development in the very choicest areas of the Sierras."

Mineral King, it was argued, is no wilderness and has not been since 1873. Its use could help preserve the actual wilderness areas from over use.

The last issue returned to the transportation problem. "The access road would put a financial burden on the state. Other more necessary roads would be neglected because of the money allocated for this road."

This concept was easy to refute. The access road would bring far more money to the state and county coffers than would be taken out. The benefits of such a resort development would affect everyone. If money was an issue, then Mineral King would have to be developed.

But the Sierra Club did not just propagandize and argue. Already, it was taking action. A National Park Service hearing was held in Fresno in November 1966 on wilderness designations in Sequoia-Kings Canyon National Park. The Sierra Club and National Parks Association asked that wilderness boundaries be mapped down to the edges of the existing Mineral King road where it ran through park land. Without right of way, the new road could not be built.

Failing to get their wilderness classification, the club started pressing for public hearings on the whole question of the resort and road, of making Mineral King a part of Sequoia National Park. The requests for hearings were not granted. There was no legal requirement for hearings and no provisions for them.

Throughout the controversy, the forces for development continued to work toward their goal. Since receiving its preliminary permit in 1966 Disney Productions had implemented a comprehensive study and planning program. Never before had the valley been studied by so many professionals. Teams comprised of specialists in each area of concern were sent in. Ecologists, geologists, hydrologists; soil scientists; winter sports planners, architects, resort operators; flood control, construction, and sanitation engineers; water rights specialists, landscape architects, snow surveyors; all probed the valley to record and report every detail that might be integral to the development of a resort.

The Forest Service gave its full cooperation, assigning Peter Wyckoff, an experienced recreation expert, to work full time with

[157]

the company's planners. Through him, Disney had access to a full range of the Department of Agriculture's technical data and experience in land management.

On January 8, 1969, the results of all the research and planning were submitted to the supervisor of the Sequoia National Forest. The "Master Plan for the Development of Mineral King" was quickly approved. On January 21 the Forest supervisor sent a letter to Disney Productions giving the stamp of approval ". . . subject to changes and further refinements as ways are found to improve it, and site development plans and detailed structure plans are yet to come."

With the approval of the master plan and funding for construction of the road through park lands assured, the opposition decided the time had come to make its major move.

On June 5, 1969, the Sierra Club, a non-profit California corporation, brought civil action against Walter J. Hickel, Secretary of Interior of the United States; John S. McLaughlin, Superintendent of Sequoia National Park; Clifford M. Hardin, Secretary of Agriculture of the United States; J. W. Deinema, Regional Forester, Forest Service; and M. R. James, Forest Supervisor, Sequoia National Forest.

The club sought both a preliminary and permanent injunction against the granting of permits, against the authorization or approval of design standards or rights of way for the Mineral King Highway, and against the construction or maintenance of such a highway.

Civil Action Number 51464 was taken before the United States District Court, Northern District of California. The defendants worked up a hurried defense, but on July 23 United States District Judge William T. Sweigert granted the preliminary injunction.

The defendants took their case to the United States Court of Appeals for the Ninth Circuit. Their case was strengthened and they received "friend of the court" aid from the U.S. Ski Association and from Tulare County. The Sierra Club sharpened its own case. Oral arguments were presented in court and the case was taken under advisement.

There the matter rested. By June 1970 no decision had yet been announced. The Sierra Club went on to other battles and activities;

fighting the construction of another dam on the Colorado River, opposing the oil pipe line through Alaska, struggling to maintain its status with the government as a non-profit, non-political corporation.

But the Mineral King development was stopped. Once again the dreams were faltering. Disney Productions suspended most of its Mineral King operations until a decision was reached, and it turned full efforts to its Florida project. The Forest Service tabled its plans. The Park Service waited.

On September 17, 1970, the Ninth Circuit Court of Appeals awarded its unanimous decision. It overruled the lower court's injunction with a 29 page decision stating that the Sierra Club lacked standing to bring suit.

The members of the Sierra Club were shocked by the decision. But they were not defeated. They pulled their forces back to the Mineral King issue and re-formed their battle lines. Within a month they had asked for a stay so they could take their case to the United States Supreme Court.


In 1969, as if to illustrate the controversy, the old resort was destroyed. Avalanches struck again. The winter of 1968-1969 was the heaviest ever recorded in Mineral King. By February more than fifteen feet of snow had covered the valley floor. On Friday, February 26, Robert Hicks, the Disney Mineral King director, ordered his snow survey teams out of the valley. With the heavy snows, a threat of new storms, and the lack of as yet adequate avalanche controls, Mineral King was in danger.

Four of six people wintering in the valley left. Wally Ballenger and Randy Kletka stayed behind; Ballenger, because he wanted to accomplish as much work as possible to complete the February report.

On Saturday a new storm came in, the highest intensity storm Ballenger reported he had ever seen. He measured the snow fall at a rate of four inches per hour. Three inches per hour is considered the disaster rate. His last survey showed the snow depth at twenty feet.

Ballenger was the former director of the ski patrol and avalanche control at Squaw Valley, so he knew the dangers. He and Kletka

*The ski country of Mineral King*

moved to separate cabins as a precautionary measure. They both closed themselves in while the storm continued.

On Monday evening, the avalanche hit. Ballenger reported it to be the worst experience he had ever endured, and he had already survived three avalanches in his 43 years.

The roar was deafening. "All I could do was pray," he said. Half the cabin in which he was staying collapsed. He tunneled to the surface of the other half, through eight feet of snow, to create an airhole. "I used my nails, a small shovel . . . I dug most the night."

It was storming again the next morning. Ballenger worked his way to the outside. He searched, sinking in snow up to his armpits when he tried to walk, but there were no signs of Kletka.

Dave Beck, one of the snow surveyors who had left on Friday, flew over the valley. Ballenger returned to his radio and made contact with the plane. On Wednesday aid came by helicopter and by foot. Ballenger was taken down to Three Rivers. The search began for Randy Kletka. He was found in Dave Beck's cabin, shovel by his side, suffocated. Mineral King's avalanches had claimed another life.

The snowslide had swept down Potato Row Hill and triggered a second one which roared down the opposite direction from Miner's Ridge. In all, that winter it was estimated that fourteen or more major avalanches hit the area.

The resort was destroyed. From Faculty Flats on up, cabins were flattened or damaged. The Green cabin, the Bartons', the Pinkham's two of the rental cabins all disappeared. And the "temporary" store and post office that Arthur Crowley had made out of two cabins pushed together in the last big avalanches of 1906 was crushed. The remnants of the past were gone. Without the store and the old resort, it would never be the same. Now there was nothing left but the future.

Those whose cabins had not been too badly damaged, returned the next spring over the washed out road. They dug out. They patched and repaired their cabins, determined to keep whatever was left to them of the valley as it was. Perhaps in another year or another decade, it would all be changed.

It took three years after the winter of 1968-1969. On Wednesday, April 19, 1972, the Supreme Court of the United States announced its decision. By a vote of four to three, it upheld the decision of the Ninth Circuit Court of Appeals. The majority opinion held that the Sierra Club was not entitled to continue its litigation as it could not show that the club itself would suffer economic or other injury from the development of the Mineral King Valley. The dissenting opinion of Justice Douglas was to help guide and motivate the forces for conservation throughout the country for years to come.

"Mineral King is doubtless like other wonders of the Sierra Nevada such as Tuolumne Meadows and the John Muir Trail," Douglas wrote in his opinion. "Those who hike it, fish it, hunt it, camp in it, or visit it merely to sit in solitude and wonderment are legitimate spokesmen for it, whether they may be a few or many. Those who have that intimate relation with the inanimate object about to be injured, polluted, or otherwise despoiled are its legitimate spokesmen.

"The voice of the inanimate object . . . should not be stilled . . . before these priceless bits of Americana (such as a valley, an alpine meadow, a river, or a lake) are forever lost or are so transformed as to be reduced to the eventual rubble of our urban environment, the voice of the existing beneficiaries of these environmental wonders should be heard."

But this was the dissenting opinion. The pro-development forces had won. Yet they greeted the news of their victory with some reservations. Once more they could work toward their ultimate dreams, but they also had to study the prospects of a new Sierra Club suit. They resumed work cautiously.

Disney Productions reaffirmed its determination ". . . to establish at Mineral King new standards of excellence in the development of recreational facilities on public land, consistent with the protection of the surrounding environment."

They renewed their efforts, tackling the problem of access to the valley. Beyond the litigation, this was the most difficult problem to be solved. More studies were made, and a decision was announced. Due to the escalating highway construction costs, and in order to reduce environmental impacts, all but eight initial miles of the existing roadway would be eliminated. The distance from Oak Grove to the "Mineral King Village" would be covered by an electric, cog-assisted railway. Construction costs of such a railway were estimated to be $53,876,000. User cost would range from five to seven dollars per round trip.

Seven years earlier, a two lane, all-weather highway had been projected to cost $25,000,000. But now, a railway at over twice the cost was being considered. The "environmental impacts" appeared to be the greatest factor in the proposal. Perhaps the elimination of the roadway would help to satisfy the environmentalists.

But it did not. As had been expected, the plaintiffs in the litigation amended their complaint. The amended lawsuit contended that the Federal Government exceeded its authority on four counts: issuing a development permit exceeding the 80 acre limitation set by Congress; granting right-of-way for a road or public conveyance medium through Sequoia National Park, when such a

[162]

roadway was not essential to Park management; not complying with the National Environmental Policy Act requirements for filing environmental statements.

The litigation returned to the U.S. Federal District Court in San Francisco. Disney Productions again put a hold on its activities in the valley. But the Forest Service, with dogged determination, continued the fight. It had far too much to lose. If it lost this battle, it could lose Mineral King.

*Foxtail Pines on Empire Mountain, some of the largest of earth's oldest living trees.*

# THIRTEEN

---◆---

# PRESERVATION

"The mountains provide variety for our lives—clean air and water, quiet solitude, uncluttered vistas and beauty. These things we prize, but they must be guarded, for they can disappear as quickly in the mountains as they have elsewhere."

Guided by this concern, expressed in one of their bulletins, the Sierra Club explored all avenues to the preservation of the Mineral King Valley. A lawsuit could delay development indefinitely, but it would not bring a change in the over-all status. If enough pressure were brought, at some time in the future Mineral King could still be turned into a major resort.

There was only one logical avenue for preservation. Mineral King must be made part of Sequoia National Park.

Since 1891 forces had been working toward this conclusion of the valley's fate. The goal of everyone involved in its history had basically been the same: to preserve Mineral King's quiet beauty and yet to let it belong to the people. Only the extent of its preservation or usage was in question.

Increasingly in the 1960s and 70s the conservationists were exerting their influence. If the Sierra Club demands seemed to overstep the bounds of practicality, they served as a tempering force. They helped to form guidelines for the conservation of all our national resources.

In the 1960s the concept of placing Mineral King within Sequoia National Park became a serious matter. As Disney Productions formulated its plans for the ultimate resort, plans to stop any development were taken before Congress. In each session, some form of legislation to change Mineral King's status was presented. Inevitably, each bill died in committee as too local a problem or as inappropriate to the needs of the area. The Disney influence and the skiing interests seemed to have the upper hand.

But the conservationists were not ones to admit defeat. To quit now would be to forever lose Mineral King as they knew it.

The Forest Service struggled to keep Mineral King in the only way in which it was experienced, through hard work. In the Sierra Club's amended suit, the one item upon which the Forest Service could act was the lack of an environmental statement.

Work was begun on a study which was published in December 1974 as the Draft Environmental Statement. The purpose of this first draft was to present to the public a preliminary report outlining a feasible development of the valley along with the possible environmental consequences of such development and with estimated costs.

The draft environmental statement was issued with a 90 day review period ending on March 31, 1975. One thousand copies of the report were printed and distributed to individuals, government agencies, organizations, legislators, Forest Service offices, universities and public libraries.

Over 2,000 comments were returned in the 90 day period, representing 4,400 signatures. Over half the responses were generated from Southern California, and most of the input came from individuals or families. Obviously, the development of Mineral King was of interest to the public.

Many of the responses gave only a pro or con reaction to the development. However, several specific concerns evolved from a Forest Service analysis: there was insufficient information to accurately assess environmental impacts; alternatives to the plan had not been clearly identified and evaluated; the draft statement failed to show conclusively that the proposal was consistent with the purposes of the Sequoia National Game Refuge; and the recreation user cost appeared to be restrictive.

With predictable thoroughness, the Forest Service implemented new studies designed to provide information that might alleviate the concerns expressed. It was, in effect, starting over again in its education of the interested public as to its goals and objectives for the valley.

In 1974 the Economic Development Administration grant expired which had set aside $3 million to the California State Highway Commission for construction of a Mineral King highway. With escalating cost figures, the grant had become nearly meaningless. Without greatly increased funding, a highway project was impossible. Nonetheless, the concept of a cog railway was prohibitive in cost. The Forest Service recommendation had to return to the feasibility of an all-season highway.

The worry about overpopulation of the valley brought a reduction in recommended visitor usage and a reduction in campground capacities. Concern over restrictive cost to the general public was considered in the elimination of the expensive cog railroad from the proposal.

In February 1976 a Final Environmental Statement was filed, incorporating the changes designed to satisfy the concerns that had been expressed. To satisfy the "enjoyment without high cost" factions, ten additional miles of trail were added to the fifteen already planned. The two lane road was proposed to terminate in parking facilities at Faculty Flat with a low cost electric bus taking visitors into the Mineral King Village. Only the eighteen ski lifts remained as originally planned, as well as the general areas of tourist facilities.

The impact on ". . . possible endangered and rare wildlife species," and other ". . . adverse environmental impacts which cannot be avoided," were also outlined in the Environmental Statement. These included increases in erosion rates, air pollution emissions, diversion of water flows, vegetation modification, loss of rural lifestyle, additional traffic and noise, visual character modification, and the loss of potential wilderness classification. None of the adverse impacts appeared to overcome the benefits of development.

[167]

"One of the responsibilities of the Forest Service is to provide a variety of the recreation opportunities and experiences to a broad cross-section of the public," one of the fact sheets explained. "Since each recreation offering cannot be all things to all people, it is our goal to present a balanced program."

In its concept of the development of Mineral King, the Forest Service felt it had presented a balanced program. Through newsletters, fact sheets, newspaper articles, it hoped to convince the public of the advisability of its program.

Confident that it had handled the major areas of concern to the best of its resources, the Department of Agriculture continued its program of education. It concluded a study of air quality control. It awaited an administrative decision on the Final Environmental Statement. It waited for the outcome of the Sierra Club litigation. It also kept a watchful eye on measures to bring Mineral King into Sequoia National Park.

A major political force was emerging in the move to incorporate Mineral King into the Park. That force was Representative John Krebs of Fresno. Joining with Representative Phillip Burton of San Francisco, Krebs brought intensive focus to the issue.

The two men were battling a time honored concept of the American way of life; economic progress. Development would encourage new revenues and job opportunities within a reportedly depressed area of the San Joaquin Valley. There were powerful groups backing the development. Not only the Disney enterprises with their millions of dollars of resources, but the skiing interests, Chamber of Commerce, even labor union groups gave their support to the development. Basically, all that conservationists had backing them was public sentiment. The preservation of wilderness was becoming a popular issue.

The Sierra Club had drawn away from the pressing need to win its lawsuit. Instead, it concentrated its energies and resources on measures to bring Mineral King into the Park System.

On March 9, 1977, U.S. District Court Judge W. T. Sweigert dismissed the amended lawsuit on grounds that the Sierra Club had failed to prosecute. However, the Forest Service greeted the news with something less than excitement.

"Although the court decision would allow the development to commence, no action will be taken until we receive a decision on the Final Environmental Statement," said Forest Supervisor John Leasure. "The decision of the former administration to proceed with development is now being reviewed by the Secretary of Agriculture and the Secretary of Interior. We are hopeful that we will be able to move forward with the Mineral King project in the near future."

The prospects were increasingly slim. Several Congressional bills were being formulated relating to the Mineral King area. Beyond that, the Wild Rivers Act had proved popular with the voting public. The trend was toward wilderness classification of undeveloped areas. A giant bill was taking shape, encompassing changes for over 75 historic and scenic areas, trails and rivers, with studies planned for the future of almost 20 more. The Mineral King issue was only one small area of concern in a national trend of preservation controversy.

California Congressmen Phillip Burton and John Krebs recognized their opportunity. Burton, as Parks subcommittee chairman, could bring a large measure of influence. A man of seemingly boundless energies, he was helping in attempts to draw nearly 100 individual environmental areas of concern into one comprehensive package. It was apparent that only with one omnibus bill could any individual area's needs be protected.

The Forest Service had no real means to battle the trend toward conservation. It could only educate the people to the fact that the Forest Service had been created to administer conservation of national resources. Conservation had been the core of its policies since its inception.

Nor did all conservationists back the concept of blocking development. The Disney Corporation had published an impressive list of the backers of development that included the president of the Wildlife Management Institute, the executive director of the National Wildlife Federation, and an associate director of the National Park Service.

But all the education, logic, money and political power could not divert the public sentiment. The wilderness was disappearing and only the people could prevent it. In April 1978 President Carter's administration agreed to support John Kreb's proposal. This was the backing Krebs and Burton needed.

On February 27 Burton's house subcommittee, in less than 15 minutes, approved Kreb's bill, to be included in the omnibus Parks bill.

The bill not only transferred 16,200 acres of the game refuge to the Park, but also outlined purchase by the federal government of 741 acres of private land holdings in the area. Studies of possible recreational facilities and road improvement were suggested. The possibility for a scaled-down ski resort was left open.

Recognizing final defeat, the Disney Corporation sent a letter to Burton requesting a "fair and equitable" reimbursement for the 1.2 million dollars in costs incurred by their company since 1965. This year of 1978 was the year their master plan was originally to have been completed. Instead they had nothing for the years, the effort and the monies they had, in good faith, expended.

Burton was unbending, saying, ". . . a company of that size and influence" had to understand, ". . . sometimes you win and sometimes you don't."

The House passed the bill on July 12 with almost no changes and without any recorded opposition. It was sent to the Senate. In the Senate version several amendments appeared, one denying compensation to the Disney Corporation; and another outlining usage by present lease holders and businesses in the area; and the most controversial amendment, denying any possibility of the construction of a ski area within the valley.

"The Congress recognizes that the Mineral King Valley area has outstanding potential for certain year-round recreational opportunities, but the development of permanent facilities for downhill skiing within the area would be inconsistent with the preservation and enhancement of its ecological values."

With this amendment included, on October 12, 1978, on one of the last days of the 95th session of Congress, by a voice vote, the omnibus Parks bill was approved. A separate bill presented by Alan Cranston of California, and which included development of skiing facilities, never reached the Senate floor.

The final decision had been made. With the signature of the President of the United States, the Mineral King Valley was preserved.

After years of struggle, of caring, planning, and administrating with a vast expenditure of public funds, the Forest Service had been relieved of its responsibilities. The future of Mineral King had been returned to the Department of Interior.

And beyond that, the future of all our national wild lands and undeveloped areas had been given direction. A century of struggle within the Mineral King Valley had helped to define on a national level a trend away from development. It had given credence to the democratic concept that people, not wealth, can direct our future.

For Mineral King, if development were to come, it would come slowly. For another generation or for many generations, people could see the valley very much as Harry O'Farrell had first seen it. It would be possible to stand in the windy pass of Farewell Gap and look out over the delicate valley; to see the undisturbed meadows and colored mountainsides, the aspens and the wildlife. To be able to imagine what the dreams and labors had been of the men and women of the past. To be able to gather into themselves the solitude, the peacefulness, the timelessness the valley represents.

The people who now came could understand what Bill Wallace had felt in 1875 when he first saw the valley.

"At the first view looking downward it appeared the most beautiful place I had ever beheld," he wrote. "Nature had worked carefully and generously in creating that scene."

Now men could work carefully to preserve that scene. Development might come and the promise of Beulah would be met. But now that promise had been defined. The wealth of this valley was not to be in her gold and silver, in her potential usage. Beulah's promise was in her beauty.

---

# APPENDIX

## A VISITOR'S GUIDE
## TO THE MINERAL KING VALLEY
### AREAS AND POINTS OF INTEREST—1978

*Camps:*
Mineral King—7,830 ft.
Faculty Flat—7,500 ft.
  (M. K. Guard Station)
Silver City—6,935 ft.
Cabin Cove
Atwell Mill—6,500 ft.
  (Campground and Ranger
  Station)
Spring Creek Campground
Sunny Point Campground
Cold Springs Campground—
  7,504 ft.
The Junipers

*Flats and Meadows:*
Aspen Flat
White Chief Meadow
Ground Hog Meadows

*Gaps and Passes:*
Timber Gap—9,400 ft.

*Gaps and Passes:*
Glacier Pass—11,600 ft.
Sawtooth Pass—11,680 ft.
Franklin Pass—11,700 ft.
Farewell Gap—10,587 ft.

*Lakes:*
Monarch
  Upper—10,638 ft.
  Lower—10,380 ft.
Crystal
  Upper—10,875 ft.
  Lower
Cobalt
  Upper—10,150 ft.
  Lower—9,900 ft.
Franklin
  Upper—10,570 ft.
  Lower—10,327 ft.
White Chief
  Big—10,390 ft.
  Little

[173]

Lakes:
Mosquitos (five)
  8,950 to 10,040 ft.
Mineral Lakes
  Silver—9,620 ft.
  Gold—9,460 ft.
  Mica—9,480 ft.
  Galena—9,625 ft.
  Quartz—9,675 ft.

Peaks and Ridges:
Juniper Ridge—10,075 ft.
Empire Mountain—11,509 ft.
Sawtooth Peak—12,343 ft.
Mineral Peak—11,550 ft.
Half Potato Hill
Rainbow Mountain—11,975 ft.
Tulare Peak—11,588 ft.
West Florence Peak—11,600 ft.
Florence Peak—12,432 ft.
Vandever Mountain—11,947 ft.
Bearskin Patch

White Chief Peak—11,050 ft.
White Chief Ridge
Vandever Ridge
Eagle Ridge
Miner's Ridge

Streams and Canyons:
Monarch Creek
Chihuahua Canyon
Crystal Creek
Franklin Creek
Farewell Canyon
White Chief Creek
Eagle Creek
Mosquito Creek
Mineral Creek
Spring Creek
East Fork Kaweah River

Falls:
Black Wolf Falls
Spring Creek
Three Falls Below The Gate

Trails:

Trails within the Mineral King area and high Sierra country are often more difficult and take longer to travel than their distances would indicate. Those within the valley make good walks or half day trips; those within the Sawtooth Circle in general are full day trips; those outside the Circle are from one hard day to several day's trips, usually pack trips. Distances given are calculated from the Mineral King camp, specifically from the old store. All distances are approximate. Those to National Park sites are estimates.

Areas within the valley:
  Soda Springs—.25 mile
  Iron Springs—.5 mile
  Cold Springs Campground—1.0 mile
  Black Wolf Falls—.6 mile
  Spring Creek—.2 mile
  Franklin Creek—2.0 miles

Areas within the Sawtooth Circle:
    Timber Gap—2.0 miles
    Farewell Gap—5.0 miles
    Monarch Lake, lower—2.75 miles
    Sawtooth Pass—3.5 miles
    Franklin Lake, lower—5.0 miles
    Franklin Pass—7.9 miles
    Crystal Lake—3.0 miles
    White Chief Meadows—2.0 miles
    White Chief Lake—2.75 miles
    Eagle Lake—3.25 miles
    Mosquito Lake No. 2—4.0 miles

Areas outside the Sawtooth Circle:
    Columbine Lake—4.0 miles
    Bullfrog Lakes—6.0 miles
    Broder Cabin—8.0 miles
    Cliff Creek—4.25 miles
    Shotgun Pass—11.0 miles
    Rattlesnake Creek—10.0 miles
    Big Kern River—16.5 miles
    Kern Lake—24.0 miles
    Moraine Lake—17.0 miles
    Five Lakes—11.0 miles
    Funston Meadow—19.0 miles
    Hockett Meadows—8.0 miles

*Lakes and Fishing:*
    The Mineral King Stream (East Fork Kaweah River) is planted with rainbow trout. Below Faculty Flats rainbow and brown trout are self-sustaining. There are twenty lakes in the Mineral King basin and sixteen contain trout.

Colbalt Lake, lower—9,900 ft.; ½ acre; 15 ft. deep; limited natural fish propagation; eastern brook.
Cobalt Lake, upper—10,150 ft.; 1 acre; 15 ft. deep; no fish.
Crystal Lake, lower—10,788 ft.; 11 acres; approx. 40 ft. deep; natural propagation; eastern brook; dammed.
Crystal Lake, upper—10,875 ft.; 2 acres; 15 ft. deep; no fish.
Eagle Lake—10,000 ft.; 12 acres; 39 ft. deep; natural propagation; eastern brook; dammed.

[175]

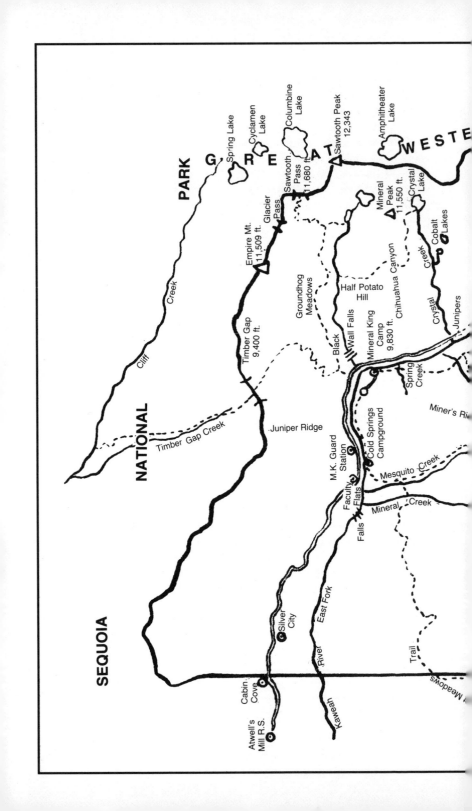

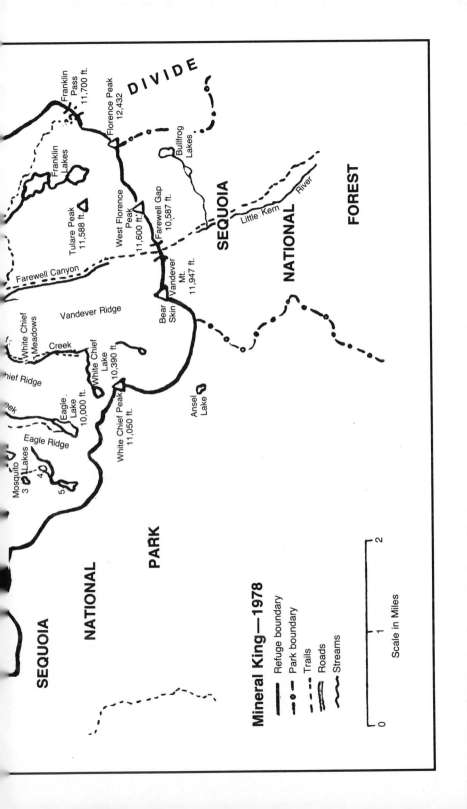

Franklin Pass 11,700 ft.

Florence Peak 12,432

D I V I D E

Franklin Lakes

Bullfrog Lakes

SEQUOIA

Tulare Peak 11,588 ft.

West Florence Peak 11,600 ft.

Farewell Gap 10,587 ft.

Little Kern River

Farewell Canyon

Vandever Mt. 11,947 ft.

NATIONAL

Vandever Ridge

Bear Skin

FOREST

White Chief Meadows

Creek

White Chief Lake 10,390 ft.

hief Ridge

White Chief Peak 11,050 ft.

Ansel Lake

Eagle Lake 10,000 ft.

ek

Eagle Ridge

Mosquito 3 Lakes

4

5

PARK

SEQUOIA

NATIONAL

**Mineral King—1978**

Refuge boundary

Park boundary

Trails

Roads

Streams

0        1        2

Scale in Miles

Franklin Lake, lower—10,327 ft.; 30 acres; natural propagation; eastern brook; dammed.

Franklin Lake, upper—10,570 ft.; 17 acres; 25 ft. deep; natural propagation; eastern brook.

Galena Lake—9,625 ft.; 2.3 acres; 12 ft. deep; periodic planting; rainbow.

Gold Lake—9,460 ft.; 1.6 acres; 7 ft. deep; natural propagation; rainbow.

Mica Lake—9,480 ft.; ½ acre; 5 ft. deep; no fish.

Monarch Lake, lower—10,380 ft.; 2.5 acres; 20 ft. deep; natural propagation; eastern brook.

Monarch Lake, upper—10,638 ft.; 16 acres; over 100 ft. deep; natural propagation; eastern brook; dammed.

Mosquito Lake No. 1—8,950 ft.; 418 acres; 11 ft. deep; natural propagation; eastern brook.

Mosquito Lake No. 2—9,580 ft.; 6 acres; 26 ft. deep; occasionally planted; eastern brook, rainbow.

Mosquito Lake No. 3—9,825 ft.; 1 acre; 9 ft. deep; natural propagation; eastern brook.

Mosquito Lake No. 4—9,925 ft.; 4 acres; 16 ft. deep; natural propagation; eastern brook.

Mosquito Lake No. 5—10,040 ft.; 10 acres; approximately 25 ft. deep; natural propagation; eastern brook.

Quartz Lake—9,675 ft.; ¾ acre; approximately 10 ft. deep; no fish.

Silver Lake—9,620 ft.; 4.2 acres; 16 ft. deep; natural propagation; rainbow.

White Chief Lake—10,390 ft.; 3.2 acres; 17 ft. deep; planted; eastern brook and rainbow.

# AREAS AND POINTS OF INTEREST—1879-1897

(Elevations differ quite markedly from those measured in more recent years. Some names correspond to areas with different names on 1970 map).

*Camps*:
Beulah—8,000 ft.
Harry's Bend or Dog Town
Empire Mill
Sunny Point
Ford's Camp or Ford's Crossing
The Gate
Below-the-Gate (now Faculty Flats)
Barton's
Weishar's Mill or Silver City
Atwell Mill
Empire Village
White Chief Camp
   (White Chief Cabin)—8,725 ft.
Nig's Cave (near the
   White Chief Mine)—9,330 ft.

*Trails*:
Timber Gap (to Cliff Creek)
Farewell Gap (to Broder's Cabin)
Tar Gap (to Hockett Meadows)
White Chief camp and mine
Empire Mine
Ford's Crossing

*Flats*:
The Flat (now Mineral King Valley)
White Chief Flats, upper and lower
Eagle Flats
Grasshopper Flats
Young America Flats (now Ground
   Hog Flats)

*Falls*:
Black Wolf Falls

Smith Falls or Spring Creek
Three-Falls-Below-the-Gate

*Peaks and Ridges*:
Empire Mountain
Empire Cliffs
Miner's Peak—12,343 ft.
   (now Sawtooth Peak)
Potato Row Mountain
   (now Half Potato Hill)
Little Matterhorn
   (now Mineral Peak)
Florence Peak
Little Florence
   (now West Florence Peak)
Bearskin
The Amphitheater
   (now White Chief Ridge or Rim)
Comanche Ridge
   (now Mineral Ridge)
Eagle Ridge

*Gaps and Passes*:
Timber Gap
Farewell Gap—10,600 ft.
Franklin Pass—11,500 ft.
McGinnis Pass—10,000 ft.
   (now Glacier or Sawtooth Pass)

*Streams and Canyons*:
Monarch Creek
Rocky Gorge Canyon
   (now Chihuahua Canyon)
Lake Canyon
   (now Crystal Creek)

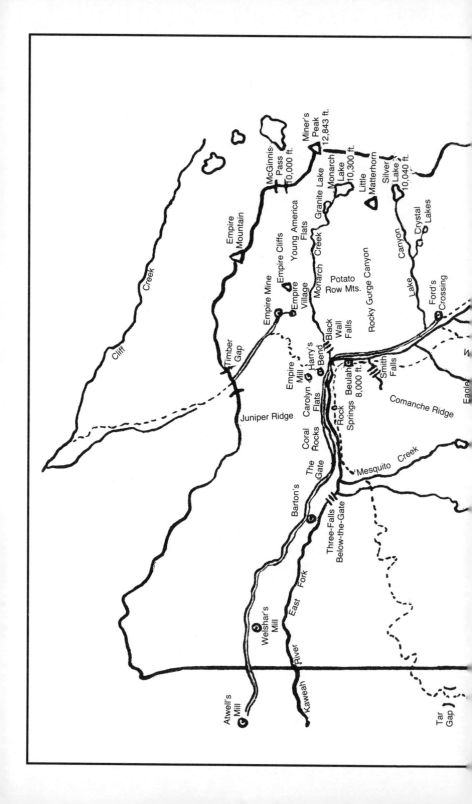

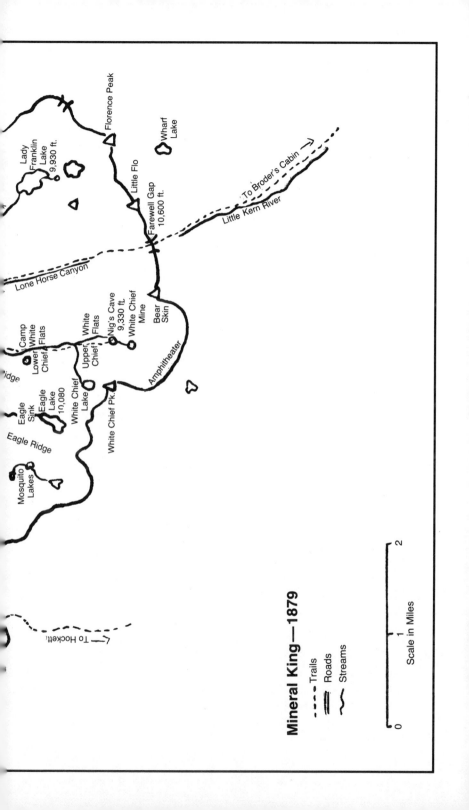

# Mineral King—1879

- - - - Trails
━━━ Roads
⌒ Streams

Scale in Miles

0        1        2

Florence Peak

Wharf Lake

Lady Franklin Lake 9,930 ft.

Little Flo

Farewell Gap 10,600 ft.

To Broder's Cabin

Little Kern River

Lone Horse Canyon

Camp White Flats

Upper White Flats

Nig's Cave 9,330 ft.

White Chief Mine

Bear Skin

Lower White Chief

Amphitheater

Ridge

White Chief Lake

Eagle Sink

Eagle Lake 10,080

White Chief Pk.

Eagle Ridge

Mosquito Lakes

To Hockett

Lady Franklin Creek
Lone Horse Canyon
   (now Farewell Canyon)
White Chief Creek
Eagle Canyon
Eagle Sink
Mosquito Canyon
Spring Creek
The Stream
   (East Fork Kaweah)

*Lakes*:
Lady Franklin—9,930 ft.
Silver Lake—10,040 ft.
   (now Crystal Lake)
Crystal Lake (now Cobalt Lake)
Monarch Lake—10,300 ft.
Granite Lake (now lower Monarch)
Eagle Lake—10,030 ft.
White Chief Lake
Mosquito Lakes

## MINES WITHIN THE MINERAL KING DISTRICT

*Important Claims—1879*:
Empire
White Chief
Chihuahua
Comanche
Cherokee
White Horse
Young America
Napoleon
Lady Franklin
Silver King
Dolly Varden
Dry Bone
Black Wolf
Black Chief
Fern Leaf
Galena Boss
Chickasaw
Anna Fox
Tonopah
Silver Tip
McGinnis

*Smaller Claims—1873-1897*:
Big Jim
Lady Emma
Lady Alice
Crowley Copper
Double Standard
Mammoth
Venice
Buckeye
Crystal
Mogul
Iron Cap
Silverite
Mankin
Rubicon
John Franklin
Florence
Silver Age
Zinc Hole

## MINERALS

The Mineral King Valley is a combination of ancient, upthrust folded seabed and younger, molten material thrust up from inside the earth. The younger formations crystallized into granite. The older, sedimentary sea formations folded and compressed into marble, slate and schist. Within them still lie fossils, especially along the eastern side of the Sawtooth Circle from Miner's Ridge to Florence Peak. Within them also lie all the ores that have tempted men since 1873. The younger granite covers and surrounds the sedimentary stratas in many areas, protecting it both from the elements and from miners.

Minerals in the Mineral King area must be quartz mined: solid quartz-bearing rock dug and blasted from a vein; crushed in a stamping mill; washed (passed over shelves of mercury or quicksilver which collects the gold and lets the crushed rock pass on); then released by distilling off the mercury. This is an expensive and slow process. In Mineral King, where the ores are heavily fused with the surrounding materials, it is especially difficult.

Leading rocks found within the Mineral King district:

| | | |
|---|---|---|
| Limestone | Calcerous Limestone | Mica Schist |
| Gneiss | Quartzite | Granite |
| Plumbaginous Schist | Slate | Quartz |

Diorite, the miner's porphyry, purplish-red, containing small crystals of feldspar

The five general classes of ore in the Mineral King district:
Sulphide of lead, or galena—common, heavy mineral, occurring in lead-gray crystals, usually cubes and cleavable masses. Galena contains gold and silver.
Sulphide of zinc, or blende—contains gold and silver in lesser qantities than the galena.
Sulphide of copper—contains copper, gold and silver.
Sulphide of iron—contains gold and silver in lesser quantities.
Arsenical iron—contains some gold and silver.
Some carbonate of lead.
Small deposits of antimony.

General area of ore within the Sawtooth Circle:
Gold, silver, zinc—higher elevations along the Great Western Divide and in the White Chief area.
Lead, silver, zinc—lower altitudes on the western side of the Sawtooth Circle, Mineral (Comanche) Ridge, etc.
Copper—lower slopes of the east side of the East Fork Canyon, e.g. Black Wolf Cave, Crowley Copper, and elevations close to the valley floor.
All ores are scattered, none apparently in any concentrated deposits.

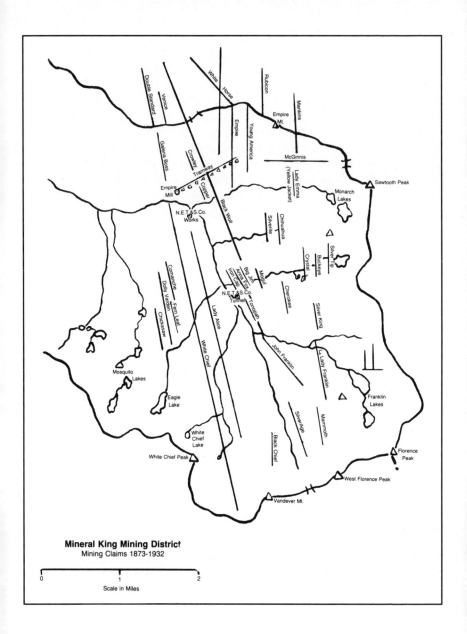

**Mineral King Mining District**
Mining Claims 1873-1932

0          1          2
Scale in Miles

# ANIMAL LIFE

Animals within the Sawtooth Circle are dependent upon altitudes, variations in plant growth, seasonal changes, and phenomena of annual variations in climate, for their means of survival and sources of existence. Beyond these natural ecological patterns, man has played a strong role in the changing structure of animal habitation in the valley.

When Harry Parole discovered the valley in 1864, he described it as filled with game totally lacking in any fear of man or guns. Mountain sheep, deer and bear were all within the valley. When Arthur Crowley went to Mineral King in 1874, he again saw and recorded the presence of abundant game, ". . . surely a paradise, full of deer, mountain sheep, bear, etc."

In the mining booms of 1874 and 1879, the prospectors depended to a great extent upon hunting for their food. Groundhog stew (a young one) was the staple of many a man's diet. Mountain sheep and wolverines were hunted. The Mule Deer became scarce. By 1882 the valley was nearly devoid of game.

In 1926 the Mineral King Valley became the Sequoia National Game Refuge, and hunting was prohibited. Within a few short years the valley was inhabited again by game, and the ecological balance began to tip to the other side. Groundhogs returned to the rocky meadows. Bear came in from the Park. An occasional wolverine was seen in the higher cirques and canyons. The deer came and multiplied until the valley was stripped of its low vegetation in bad winters. The Forest Service had to open the refuge to occasional deer hunts in order to maintain the ecological balance of the valley.

Before the period of mining and until the early 1900s, fur-bearing animals were caught by trappers along the East Fork. Lines were set each winter between Atwell's Mill and the lower forested part of Mineral King and up into the Mosquito Lakes. Even now, in the summer, some fur-bearing animals can be seen along the creeks and marshes of the valley.

Some fur-bearing animals that can be found within the Mineral King area include the short-tailed Weasel, the Sierra Marten, and occasionally, the Mink and the Fisher.

Animals hunted by the miners and early settlers for food or for protection against their marauding habits, became nearly extinct in the valley by 1880. Those that did not return include the Mountain Sheep, Timber Wolf, Bob-Cat, and Grizzly Bear. The Wolverine returned only rarely.

Those that did return include the Mule Deer, Black Bear, Mountain Lion, Mountain Coyote, American Porcupine, Mountain Beaver, and the Marmot or ground hog.

Smaller animals and rodents that inhabit the Mineral King area include the White-tailed Jack Rabbit, Pika (coney or rock-rabbit), Western Gray Squirrel (Pine Squirrel), California Ground Squirrel (digger squirrel), Douglas Squirrel, Golden-mantled Ground Squirrel, Lodgepole Chipmunk, Meadow Jumping Mouse, Bush-tailed or White-throated Wood Rat (Pack Rat or Trader Rat).

Reptile life in the Mineral King area is sparse. There are no rattlesnakes in the valley. They confine themselves to the lower mountain regions and foothills. Within the valley can be found these reptiles; the Gopher Snake (Bull Snake), Garter Snakes (water snakes), and the Rubber Boa or two-headed snake which the miners bought to cure their delirium tremens.

The predominant birds in the area include Mountain Quail; an occasional California or Valley Quail; Blue Grouse (Dusky or Mountain Grouse); the Nutcracker of Clark's Crow; Golden Eagle; Red-tailed Hawk; Swainson's Hawk; several blackbirds, among them the Red-winged, the Yellow-headed, and the Brewer's Blackbird; Bullock's Oriole or Sunshine Oriole; Stellar Jay or Whiskey Jack as it was known to the miners; Rufous-sided Towhee; Red-shafted Flicker; Pileated Woodpecker; Violet-green Swallow; Tree Swallow; Mountain Chickadee; Chestnut-backed Chickadee; Robin; Western Tanager; Rufous Hummingbird; Calliope Hummingbird; and the Water Ouzel or Dipper.

## PLANT LIFE

Vegetation within the Sawtooth Circle follows no logical pattern or sequence. Plants that should be found only in the lower meadows exist in the high cirques, stunted and discolored. Those that flourish on the western side of the circle exist only in small, isolated clumps on the eastern side, while those that predominate on the eastern Great Western Divide are rare on the West slopes. At the same elevation, in different areas, can be found chaparral foliage and dense forest. For ease of identification, it is convenient to describe the vegetation according to the *general* area of predominance.

### Trees

Eastern Side (Great Western Divide):

For the most part, trees along this area are only in small clusters or sparsely spread. Two exceptions are the forest extending up the lower part of Franklin Canyon and the forested area of Timber Gap. They are fairly dense and consist of trees generally identified with the western side of the

[186]

valley. More typical of the east side are these trees: Western or Sierra Juniper, usually stunted and scrubby but growing to sixty-five feet in height as at the head of the valley Foxtail Pine, three of the largest known living found in a grove on Empire Mountain; Lodgepole Pine, called Tamarack by the old miners as it existed in its scrubby, wind beaten form on the east side of the Sawtooth Circle. Western White Pine and Red Fir grow at the higher elevations mixed with the Foxtail Pine and Lodgepole.

Western Side:

The Lodgepole Pine is most prevalent on the western side of the Sawtooth Circle, growing in dense forests. In this milder region, the trunks grow tall and straight, up to 150 ft. in height, and the old timers called the tree a lodgepole, not a tamarack.

All of the western side is heavily forested except for the higher alpine regions of the White Chief, Eagle and Mosquito bowls, and Vandever Mountain. Other trees which predominate in the lower forested areas include: the Big Tree or Sequoia Gigantea, growing generally from the 3,500 ft. to 8,400 ft. level with the highest grove on the East Fork just above Atwell's Mill; Red Fir; White or Silver Fir; Douglas Fir or Douglas Spruce; Sugar Pine; Western White Pine; Jeffrey Pine; Quaking Aspen.

Valley Floor:

The trees surrounding the Mineral King Valley sweep down from the mountainsides into the edge of the valley or form in clusters along the floor. Red Fir, Jeffrey Pine, Lodgepole Pine, Junipers, and Quaking Aspen can all be found on the valley floor.

## Shrubs

Northern and Eastern Side:

The areas below Juniper Ridge, Timber Gap, Empire Mountain, and all along the lower slopes of the Great Western Divide, sustain plant life more closely connected with chaparral than forest regions. These areas are west and south facing and lack the sustained moisture to carry a more lush plant life. Shrubs within this area include Sierra Chinquapin, Green Manzanita, Indian Manzanita, Buck Brush, Bear Brush or Silk Tassel, Mountain or High Sierra Sagebrush.

Western Side:

The western slopes carry some sagebrush and manzanita. However, more shade and moisture loving plants are able to be sustained within the forests. These include Deer Brush, Mountain Maple or Dwarf Maple,

Mountain Alder, Bridal Wreath (Mountain Spiraea or Steeple-bush), California Wild Rose, Wild Cherry (Sierra Cherry, Bitter or Red Cherry), Thimbleberry, Gooseberries, Sierra Currant, Red Elderberry, and Twinberry.

Valley Floor:
As with the trees, shrubs surrounding the valley floor creep down to it, up to it, and along it. Mountain Sage, Manzanita, Wild Roses, Wild Cherry, the Alder, Deerbrush, Buckbrush, and the different berries, all can be found in the valley. The tallest and most predominant shrub on the valley floor is the willow, although it can be found in every part of the Sawtooth Circle and down the canyon along any wet area.

## Wildflowers

Alice Eastwood, former Curator of the Museum of Natural Science, made a visit to Mineral King and was astonished at the number of flowers she classified there—nearly 300 varieties. Other people of the area, Nora Pogue Montgomery especially, have become authorities in their own rights on Mineral King flora. In a book of this nature it would be impossible to list so many plants. The flowers mentioned here are those Alice Crowley Jackson found most common and grew to know throughout the 60 summers she spent in the valley. They are listed according to general area of predominance within the Mineral King Flats and surrounding area:

Marshes and Streamside

Whitish to greenish:
False-Hellebore (Corn Lily or Skunk Cabbage); Western Solomon's Seal; Queen Anne's Lace; Cow Parsnip or Wild Parsley; Green Gentian.
Yellow-Orange-Cream:
Sierra Lily; Small Tiger Lily (Alpine Lily); Black-Eyed or Brown-Eyed Susan; California Cone Flower; Goldenrod; Buttercup.
Reddish to Pink:
Shooting Star (Cyclamen or Rooster Heads); Wild Geranium; Indian Paintbrush (Painted Cup); Mimulus (Scarlet Monkey Flower); Wild or Swamp Onion; Elephants' Heads.
Blue to Violet:
Violet; American Cowslip or Shooting Star; Sierra Gentian; Blue or Explorer's Gentian; Felwort or Purple Gentian; Mountain Bluebells

(Languid Ladies or Lungwort); Western Mountain Aster; Camas or Wild Hyacinth; Monkshood; Larkspur.

## Drier Areas

Whitish to Greenish:
Mariposa Lily (White Mariposa); Baby's Breath (Gysophila).
Yellow-Orange-Cream:
Buckwheat.
Reddish to Pink:
Pussy-Paws or Cat-Paws; Fireweed (Willow Herb or Alaskan Flame); Penstemon of several species; Scarlet Gilia.
Blue to Violet:
Blue Flax (Wild Flax); two species of Lupine, the Brewer Lupine which grows low to the ground and another which grows up to three feet in height.

## Wooded Areas

Whitish to Greenish:
Wild Cucumber or Chilicothe; Western Solomon's Seal.
Yellow-Orange-Cream:
Pine Violet (Yellow Wood Violet).
Reddish to Pink:
Miner's Lettuce (Indian Lettuce or Squaw Cabbage); Scarlet or Red Columbine; Snow Plant.
Blue to Violet:
Wild Ginger (Californian HeartLeaf); Purple Nightshade; Forget-Me-Not

## Alpine Meadows

The higher meadows and alpine cirques above Mineral King carry their own special plant life. Where plants have crept up from the lower valley and streams, they grow in stunted, paler forms. Those growing in the alpine areas that also grow in the valley areas include Penstemon, Wild Flax, Fireweed, Gentian, Bridal Wreath, Aster, Paintbrush, Mimulus, Lupine, Shooting Stars, Butter Cup, Larkspur, and Forget-me-nots.

Other plants or species not commonly found at lower elevations include:

[189]

Yellow-Orange-Cream:

Yellow Columbine (Alpine Columbine), the first of this species discovered in 1880 on Sawtooth Peak (then Miner's Peak).

Reddish to Pink:

Red Mountain Heather; Sierra Primrose; Red Snow or Protococcus nivalis, a minute plant which creates pink color on summer snow fields.

Blue to Violet:

Alpine Daisy (Lavender Mountain daisy or Fleabane); Western Pennyroyal.

Shrubs:

Two shrubs are predominant in the alpine areas. One is the High Sierra Sagebrush growing to 10,000 ft. elevations in stunted form. The other is the Alpine Willow which grows only two to four inches high.

## Ferns

Ferns grow predominantly in the shaded and moist areas of the western slopes and along the streams. Some found within the valley include: Horsetail rush (Common Horsetail or Boreale), Bracken or Brake Fern; Lady Fern; Woodwardia, the largest fern in the Mineral King area; Parsley Fern, which grows up to 10,000 ft. in granite crevices.

# ACKNOWLEDGMENTS

Alice Crowley Jackson—researcher, writer, critic; information and preliminary writing for the historical background.

Grace Alles—historical background and characters of the mining era.

Daisy Hopping—historical information on trails, stages, and packing concessions.

Peter J. Wyckoff, Mineral King Staff Specialist, Sequoia National Forest—information on national forest policy, mining data, trails, historical information, snow surveys, wild life information.

Charles R. Pickering, Acting Public Information Officer, Sequoia National Forest—information on the Final Environmental Statement, February 1976; the Sierra Club lawsuit; bills for Mineral King inclusion in Sequoia National Park, 1978.

Robert B. Hicks, Walt Disney Productions—information on Disney resort development plans and the Sierra Club suit.

Congressman John Krebs—House of Representatives' version of National Parks and Recreation Act, 1978.

Senator S. I. Hayakawa—Senate version of National Parks and Recreation Act, 1978, S.791 with final amendments.

Department of Interior—historical material.

Department of Agriculture—historical material.

Idaho State Historical Society—information on Harry Trauger.

Mrs. H. D. Dowell—information on the 1930 mining era.

Arthur Lewis Crowley—information on the Crowley era.

Nadine Crowley Graham—information on the Crowley era and general critical evaluation and aid.

Kathryn Laney Veazey—invaluable help and critical evaluation.

Barbara Buckman Hansen—information and aid on the Buckman era.

[191]

# BIBLIOGRAPHY

*MANUSCRIPTS AND DOCUMENTS:*

"Archaeological Resources of the Mineral King District"— C. H. Jennings and Patricia Kisling; U.S. Dept. of Agriculture; Jan. 1971.

Civil Action No. 51464—complaint; defendants' memorandum; memorandum of decision; brief for appellants; reply brief for appellants; briefs of amicus curiae on behalf of U.S. Ski Association, Far West Ski Association, and County of Tulare; brief for the appellee.

Civil Action No. 24966—memorandum of decision of U.S. Court of Appeals for the Ninth Circuit.

Deposition of Thomas Fowler—San Francisco: April 3, 1884.

Diaries of Arthur Crowley—1877-1931.

Diaries of John Crowley—1870-1873.

"Guardian of Sequoia National Park" petition—Dec. 15, 1894.

H.R. Act 12536, 95th Congress, Second Session; Parks and Recreation Act of 1978; U.S. House of Representatives.

Memoirs of O. D. Barton—Devil's Den; August 22, 1905.

"Mineral King History"—Gertrude Knapp; Walt Disney Productions; unpublished.

Mineral King resort brochures—1922-1978.

Mining Assays—1873-1930.

Mining claims and location notices—1873-1937.

Mining options: T. J. and W. H. Crabtree to W. F. Cord, Aug. 5, 1912; Crowley, Crabtree and Cord to Mrs. O. B. Howard, Aug. 26, 1918; Cord, Crabtree and Crowley to Interstate Industrial and Transportation Co., Oct. 23, 1929.

"Plant Checklist for Mineral King, California"—Barbara Rice; U.S. Dept. of Agriculture; Porterville, Calif., 1969.

S. 791; National Parks and Recreation Act of 1978 with final amendments; U.S. Senate.

Supreme Court of the United States Syllabus; Sierra Club vs. Morton, Secretary of the Interior, et al.; No. 70-34; argued Nov. 17, 1971; decided April 19, 1972.

The Biography of Arthur Crowley, 1931.

"The Silver Rush at Mineral King, California, 1873-1882 (portions of)—S. Thomas Porter; Visalia Calif.; a master's thesis.


*LETTERS*:

Letters concerning suit, U.S. Govt. vs. Arthur Crowley, from Dept. of Interior, U.S. Land Office and the U.S. Dept. of Agriculture, Forest Service—May 1904 through Dec. 1907.

Letters from Emma Crowley—1897-1899.

Letters from Len Cutler—1906.

Letters from Mary Trauger—1892-1931.

Letter from Professor Jackson, Professor of Geology, University of California, Berkeley, to W. B. Wallace—1897.

Letters from the National Clean-up and Paint-up Campaign Bureau; New York, to Arthur Crowley, Nov. 1928-Feb. 1929.

Letter to Mr. H. D. Dowell from Joseph V. Flynn, Assistant Regional Forester, Sequoia National Forest—Aug. 6, 1963.


*PHOTO CREDITS*:

All photographs in the book were taken from the files of Arthur Crowley with the exception of the following:

Harry's Bend—Disney Productions

Sawtooth Peak, winter of 1949—U.S. Forest Service

Ten-stamp quartz mill typical of the Empire Mill—Disney Productions

The ski country of Mineral King—Disney Productions

Winter 1949, on top of the Big Rock—U.S. Forest Service

Ray and Gem Buckman—Barbara and Jack Hansen


*BOOKS*:

Armstrong, Margaret, and J. J. Thornber. *Fieldbook of Western Wild Flowers*. New York: G. P. Putnam and Sons, 1915.

Boerker, Richard H. D. *Behold Our Green Mansions*. Chapel Hill: University of North Carolina Press, 1945.

Bowers, Nathan A. *Cone-Bearing Trees of the Pacific Coast*. Palo Alto: Pacific Books, 1956.

Brown, Vinson, and Robert Livezey. *The Sierra Nevadan Wildlife Region*. Healdsburg: Naturegraph Publishers, 1962.

Bruun, Bertel, Chandler S. Robbins, and Herbert S. Zim. *Birds of North America*. New York: Golden Press, Inc., 1966.

Caughey, John W. *California*. New York: Prentice-Hall, Inc., 1953.

Frome, Michael. *Whose Woods These Are*. New York: Doubleday, 1962.

Hacker, Louis M., and Helene S. Zahler. *The United States in the 20th Century*. New York: Appleton-Century-Crofts, Inc., 1952.

Leadabrand, Russ. *A Guide Book to the Southern Sierra Nevada*. Los Angeles: The Ward Ritchie Press, 1968.

Lee, William Storrs. *The Sierra*. New York: G. P. Putnam and Sons, 1962.

McClellan, R. Guy. *West of the Rocky Mountains*. Philadelphia: William Flint and Co., 1872.

Monaghan, Jay (ed.). *The Book of the American West*. New York: Julian Messner, Inc., 1963.

Muir, John. *The Mountains of California*. Boston and New York: Houghton Mifflin Co., 1916.

Munz, Philip A. *California Mountain Wildflowers*. Berkeley and Los Angeles: University of California Press, 1963.

Peattie, Roderick (ed.). *The Sierra Nevada*. New York: Vanguard Press, Inc., 1947.

Storer, Tracy, I., and Robert L. Usinger. *Sierra Nevada Natural History*. Berkeley and Los Angeles: University of California Press, 1963.

Tulare County. *History of Tulare County, 1883*. San Francisco: Wallace W. Elliott and Co., Publishers, 1883.

*MAGAZINES, JOURNALS AND PAMPHLETS:*

"A Few Facts About Tulare County," Tulare County Chamber of Commerce, 1959.

Adler, Pat, *Mineral King Guide*, Glendale: La Siesta Press, 1963.

*The American Ski Annual*, 1935-1936.

"Angler's Guide to the Mineral King Area," California State Department Fish and Game, November 1966.

Buckman, Mrs. Ray, "Mineral King," *The Kaweah Magazine*, August 1960.

Challacombe, J. R., "Teller of Tall Tales," *Fortnight Magazine*, November 1955.

Christensen, Mark N., "Structure of Metamorphic Rocks at Mineral King," Berkeley and Los Angeles, University of California Press, 1963.

"The Disney World," Walt Disney Production, Vol. 6, No. 1, April 1968.

Dudley, William R., "Near the Kern's Grand Cañon," *Sierra Club Bulletin*, Vol. 4, No. 4, June 1903.

*Final Environmental Statement Mineral King Recreation Development, Sequoia National Forest.*

Gibson, James N., and Ludvig J. Hasher, "Mineral King, Sequoia National Forest Winter Survey, 1947-48," 1948.

*The Golden Trout of the Southern High Sierras*, Washington, D.C.: Department of Commerce and Labor, Bureau of Fisheries, Government Printing Office, 1906.

Haskell, Burnett G., "Kaweah, How and Why the Colony Died," *Our West Magazine*, September 1902.

Hyde, Philip, "The Use of Nature," *Sierra Club Bulletin*, Vol. 43, No. 9, November 1958.

Jackson, Alice C., "A Country of Live Ghosts," *Touring Topics*, August 1924.

Leadabrand, Russ, "What About Mineral King?" *American Forests Magazine*, February 1967.

"Los Tulares," Tulare County Chamber of Commerce, Visalia, October 1952.

"Mineral King at the Crossroads," *Outdoor Newsletter*, Sierra Club, Vol. 5, No. 1, May 19, 1969.

McCloskey, Michael, "Why the Sierra Club Opposes Development of Mineral King," *Sierra Club Bulletin*, November 1967.

"Prospectus for a Proposed Recreational Development at Mineral King in the Sequoia National Forest," Forest Service, U.S. Dept. of Agriculture, California Region, February 1965.

"Report of the Acting Superintendent of the Sequoia and General Grant National Parks, California," Washington, D.C.: Government Printing Office, 1897.

*Sequoia National Forest News*, Air Quality Study Report, January 7, 1977.

[196]

*Sequoia National Forest News*, Fact Sheets, numbers 1 through 8, February 26, 1976.

*The Sunset Route Tourist Guide and Immigrants Land Directory from New Orleans to San Francisco*, San Francisco: Atwell and Co., January 1888.

Walker, E. Cordon, President, Walt Disney Productions, *Disney News*, Visalia: May 3, 1972.

Walt Disney Productions Release, August 31, 1965.

Walt Disney Productions Release, April 19, 1972.


*NEWSPAPERS*: 1891-1979

*Christian Science Monitor*: Jan. 13, 1966

*Exeter Sun*: Jan. 13, 1905; Sept. 7, 1939; Sept. 29, 1949; July 6, 1960; Aug. 10, 1960; Sept. 30, 1965; Oct. 14, 1965; Jan. 20, 1966.

*Far West Ski News*: Vol. 10, No. 7; Nov. 15, 1978.

*Fresno Bee*: Aug. 8, 1923; July 29, 1924; Aug. 9, 1924; July 23, 1962; Sept. 1, 1965; Sept. 5, 1965; Feb. 28, 1978; July 13, 1978.

*Fresno Republican*: July 18, 1926; Apr. 17, 1927; June 23, 1928.

*Hanford Sentinel*: Sept. 1, 1965; Sept.17, 1965.

*Monterey Herald*: Oct. 29, 1965; Apr. 3, 1967.

*Nevada State Journal*: Feb. 10, 1970; May 20, 1970; April 20, 1972; Oct. 17, 1978.

*Oakland Tribune*: Aug. 19, 1965; Sept. 16, 1965.

*Reno Evening Gazette*: Sept. 18, 1970.

*San Francisco Chronicle*: Oct. 28, 1965.

*Sequoia Sentinel*: July 19-25, 1978.

*Tulare County Times*: July 20, 1891.

*Visalia Daily Times*: Oct. 3, 1905; Nov. 9, 1905; Aug. 10, 1907; Oct. 12, 1907; Feb. 21, 1909; Dec. 11, 1911; Jan. 24, 1916.

*Visalia Delta*: "History of the Kaweah Colony, 1885-1891; George W. Stewart; Nov.-Dec., 1891.

Visalia Times-Delta: Jan. 3, 1929; June 5, 1931; May 5, 1948; Nov. 20, 1948; Jan. 24, 1949; Sept. 28, 1949; Jan. 27, 1951; Oct. 31, 1952; Nov. 27, 1956; June 25, 1959; Jan. 3, 1963; Oct. 9, 1965; Dec. 17, 1965; June 24, 1967.

# INDEX

Alles, Henry, 92, 104, 107
Alpine Club, 118
Alpine Creek, 7
Anderson, Bill, 7, 14, 35
Askin, Al, 127
Askin, Fred, 127
Assays, Empire, 36
Assays, White Chief, 35
Assays, 1880s, 81; 1979, 35, 36, 46, 48
Assessments, Mining 1876, 28, 29
Atwell, Judge A. J., 83
Atwell Mill, 16, 83, 94, 95, 104, 126

Baggs, Samuel, 120, 121
Baker, Charles, 28–31
Baker, John, 149
Baker, P. Y., 40
Ballenger, Wally, 159, 160, 161
Barthel, Kurt, 142
Barton, Bob, 93
Barton, Camp, 23
Barton, Enos, 17, 28–31, 58
Barton, James, 58
Barton, Jason, 58
Barton, Orlando, 28–31, 58–59, 74
Barton, Stephen, 58
Baulderas, Ray, 148
Beck, Dave, 150, 159–160
Beck, Susan, 150
Beinhorn, C. A., 122
Beldon, Charles, 8–11, 13
Beldon, Sam, 44, 71
Bequette, Pasquel, 18
Beulah, Name, 18, 42

Beulah, 1874–1878, 20–31
Bevins, 28, 29
Bids, Skiing 1949, 145
Bids, Skiing 1965, 147–150
Blair, Alice, 150
Blair, John, 150
Blossom, Charley, 91
Boer War, 103
Bollenbacher, Don, 148
Brandt, Robert, 146, 147
Broder, Jim, 104
Brown, George "Bally", 26–31
Buckman, Gem, 131, 146
Buckman, Phillip, 131
Buckman, Ray, 131–135, 143, 145, 147
Bullion, 28–29, 67
Burton, Phillip, 168–170

Cabins, 1870s, 12, 22–24, 45–46, 58;
    1890s, 90–91; 1906, 108, 110; 1920s,
    116, 117, 121, 128; 1930s, 132; 1950s,
    134, 135; 1960s, 161
Cain's Flat, 27, 37, 87, 90
California, Conservation, 84, 86–87
California Ski Association, 141
California, 1880s, 79–81; 1890s, 89, 90;
    1900s, 115, 116, 118
Camps, 1874, 16, 17, 23; 1879, 42,
    43–44, 48; 1900s, 87; 1930s, 132;
    1960s, 154
Carrington, George, 40
Carter, President, 169
Cave, Clough, 76
Cave, Nig's, 11, 17–18

[200]